T0286803

Cambridge Elements ☰

Elements in Shakespeare and Pedagogy
edited by
Liam E. Semler
The University of Sydney
Gillian Woods
Birkbeck College, University of London

THE PEDAGOGY OF WATCHING SHAKESPEARE

Bethan Marshall
King's College London

Myfanwy Edwards
University College London

Charlotte Dixey
Twyford Church of England High School

CAMBRIDGE
UNIVERSITY PRESS

Shaftesbury Road, Cambridge CB2 8EA, United Kingdom

One Liberty Plaza, 20th Floor, New York, NY 10006, USA

477 Williamstown Road, Port Melbourne, VIC 3207, Australia

314–321, 3rd Floor, Plot 3, Splendor Forum, Jasola District Centre,
New Delhi – 110025, India

103 Penang Road, #05–06/07, Visioncrest Commercial, Singapore 238467

Cambridge University Press is part of Cambridge University Press & Assessment,
a department of the University of Cambridge.

We share the University's mission to contribute to society through the pursuit of
education, learning and research at the highest international levels of excellence.

www.cambridge.org
Information on this title: www.cambridge.org/9781009114974

DOI: 10.1017/9781009118743

© Bethan Marshall, Myfanwy Edwards and Charlotte Dixey 2024

This publication is in copyright. Subject to statutory exception and to the provisions
of relevant collective licensing agreements, no reproduction of any part may take
place without the written permission of Cambridge University Press & Assessment.

When citing this work, please include a reference to the DOI 10.1017/9781009118743

First published 2024

A catalogue record for this publication is available from the British Library.

ISBN 978-1-009-11497-4 Paperback
ISSN 2632-816X (online)
ISSN 2632-8151 (print)

Cambridge University Press & Assessment has no responsibility for the persistence
or accuracy of URLs for external or third-party internet websites referred to in this
publication and does not guarantee that any content on such websites is, or will
remain, accurate or appropriate.

The Pedagogy of Watching Shakespeare

Elements in Shakespeare and Pedagogy

DOI: 10.1017/9781009118743
First published online: April 2024

Bethan Marshall
King's College London

Myfanwy Edwards
University College London

Charlotte Dixey
Twyford Church of England High School

Author for correspondence: Bethan Marshall, Bethan.marshall@klc.ac.uk

ABSTRACT: The pedagogy of acting out Shakespeare has been extensive. Less work has been done on how students learn through spectatorship. This Element considers how students learn through spectatorship within the current context of Shakespeare teaching in schools. Using grounded research, it includes work undertaken on a school's National Theatre production of *Macbeth*, as well as classroom-based, action research using a variety of digital performances of Shakespeare plays. Both find means of extending student knowledge in unexpected ways through encountering interpretations of Shakespeare that the students had not considered. In reflecting on the practice of watching Shakespeare in an educational context – both at the theatre and in the classroom – this Element hopes to offer suggestions for how teachers might rethink the ways in which they present Shakespeare performed to their students, particularly as a powerful way of building personal and critical responses to the plays.

KEYWORDS: reader response, spectator theory, powerful knowledge, *Macbeth*, *Hamlet*

© Bethan Marshall, Myfanwy Edwards and Charlotte Dixey 2024

ISBNs: 9781009114974 (PB), 9781009118743 (OC)
ISSNs: 2632-816X (online), 2632-8151 (print)

Contents

1 Introduction

The teaching of Shakespeare's plays became mandatory in England in 1989 (DES, 1989) and has remained so ever since. In two national curricula – the first in 1989, and the current one introduced in 2014 (DfE, 2014) – he is the only named author. At present students have to study at least two plays between the ages of eleven and fourteen and one play from fourteen to sixteen, typically for examination. He dominates the English curriculum in the secondary sector, replete with cultural capital. This is seen as oppressive by some (Coles, 2013a, 2013b, 2020) while others laud it (Gove, 2010; Lawson, cited in Lister, 1993). Studying him is fraught, a wrestle between many positions, which, in part, depends on whether he is considered as predominantly a playwright or attention is focused on his plays as printed texts. And on that subject the English curriculum in schools is torn, on the one hand viewing him as a dramatist and on the other, for example, exploring the richness of the language within the text. (This is also true in higher education. See Lukas Erne's *Shakespeare As Literary Dramatist*, 2013.)

In this Element, however, we take a different view. We focus on how it is possible to watch Shakespeare pedagogically, the teacher allowing the students to consider themselves as an audience of a performance, as spectators of the Shakespeare play they are viewing. They are not simply being shown a Shakespeare play; they are actively watching it, asked to think and comment on it. In so doing we see how this approach enables the students to engage with the texts, learn from the experience and create their own meaning from the play.

Students encounter performances of Shakespeare texts in a number of different ways. They can see a performance in the theatre; they can see a digital performance of a theatre production; they can watch a Theatre in Education production at the school; they can watch a film version of a play; they can view extracts of a film or a digital version of a theatre performance. Typically they do a variety of these. The nature of the performance, the choice of cast, the direction – all these will affect the watchers and create meaning from their encounter (Escolme, 2005).

We look at the experience of two practising teachers and the moments when they explore watching Shakespeare pedagogically as opposed to simply showing the play. How they watch the play may differ, in a theatre, in a school hall or digitally in the classroom, but each viewing experience is typical of the kind of encounters students might have with a play. Myfanwy Edwards is completing a PhD on a National Theatre production of *Macbeth* specifically designed for schools. The students come from five different schools (three are in the London area and two are outside of London in South East England and South Yorkshire). All were studying the play for GCSE, the examination for sixteen-year-olds, and had studied the text in detail in their respective classes. All watched a complete performance of the play, though students from one school watched it at the National Theatre while the students from the other four schools watched it at their respective schools. Her work is based on post-viewing focus groups.

Charlotte Dixey, perhaps more typically, uses film versions of *Hamlet* when teaching her A-level class (the examination for eighteen-year-olds). Her English department has in the past concentrated heavily on textual interpretations of the play rather than considering it as a drama. She was asked to revise a scheme of work (SoW) for her department, in particular the section of the exam rubric which focused on the mandatory teaching of critical theory in relation to the play. Amongst other things, she explores how watching different interpretations of the play lends itself to enabling students to recognise how various theorists understand the play (Semenza, 2003).

Dilemmas with the Current Climate: A Knowledge-Rich Curriculum

As we shall see, both teachers examine the pedagogy of watching Shakespeare's plays. Students are encouraged to confront, interpret and understand them in their role as spectators. The play text becomes open to multiple meanings and we will link this later to spectator theory. The current trend in England, however, differs and is more focused on 'core knowledge', which can be problematic. It is important to note, however, before we begin, that at no point are we advocating that knowledge is unimportant. Rather it is the way the knowledge-rich curriculum can be exemplified, the pedagogy attached, that causes a dilemma for those considering a different method of teaching. So we start by looking at the knowledge-rich curriculum and move to spectator theory afterwards.

The 'knowledge-rich curriculum' has gained increasing sway within schools in England, the US and Australia. A version of it began with the American E. D. Hirsch's (1987) book *Cultural Literacy*, in which he outlined what he thought students should 'know' when leaving school, including a canon of literature with which they should be familiar. He purports that his aims are progressive in that he believes it is the task of those involved in education to give all pupils the 'intellectual capital' that at present only a few possess. He aims to equalise society by giving the culture of a powerful minority to everybody.

The phrase 'cultural literacy' has now been replaced by 'knowledge-rich' in popular discourse, the media and government policy in England. Yet the link between 'culture' and 'knowledge' is all too evident in Conservative Party, right-leaning thinking (Yandell, 2017). Nick Gibb, former Conservative Minister of State for Education, writing a defence of Hirsch, highlights the tension, saying that the new curriculum, introduced in 2014 (DfE, 2014), was 'derided by one critic as "rote-learning of the patriotic stocking fillers", as if all that was driving us was a desire that schoolchildren celebrate the glories of the British Empire' (Gibb, 2015: 15). Absent for that 'critic' is any writer other than those who are white and British born. Given that Michael Gove, former Secretary of State for Education, had previously given a list of dead white, almost entirely British men who should be studied, the comments of the 'critic' are not surprising. Gibb argues, however: 'In reality, our reforms were based on a desire to see social justice through equalising the unfair distribution of intellectual capital in British society. Unlike so many other inequalities, this is one that schools – if performing their function properly – have the power to address' (15). He adds that 'Hirsch's arguments provided us with a compelling social justice case with which to argue for a knowledge-rich curriculum' (15).

Yet much of the problem for Shakespeare, even if we allow for the claimed motivation of 'social justice', which is highly questionable, lies in the way he is positioned within this debate. This positioning, for the Tories at least, is one of 'cultural heritage' as Brian Cox named it in the first national curriculum for English and before that in the Bullock Report (DES, 1975). Ken Jones (1989), in his book *Right Turn: The Conservative Revolution in Education*, highlights the way in which the Conservative government has consistently used the canon, and in particular Shakespeare, to herald a return to teaching 'our culture' as opposed to anything else. John Marenbon (1987), a member of the right-wing think tank the Centre for Policy Studies, wrote in *English Our English*, for example: 'A good teacher should be sceptical of originality in response to literature because it is most likely to betray a failure of understanding. The competent reader reads a work of literature much as any other competent readers read it' (37, cited in Coles, 2013b: 33).

When David Pascall, himself a chemical engineer, was given the job of rewriting the national curriculum for English after Cox was accused of 'going native' (Marshall, 2000: 12), he firmly placed the canon – and with it Shakespeare – at the centre of the English curriculum. Jane Coles analyses in some depth his 1992 speech to the Royal Society of Arts. In it, she writes, he

> [m]akes his position clear in terms of how he regarded the relationship between culture, nation and education. On the one hand Pascall acknowledges today's students will have 'a range of cultural experiences' (1992, p.16); on the other he repeatedly talks of 'our' culture, or 'a' culture and asserts that 'we' all 'share a set of values and traditions which has been developed over the centuries' (p.5). Not surprisingly, those 'important strands from our culture' which 'define and enrich our present way of life' are 'of the Christian faith, the GrecoRoman influence, the liberal Enlightenment' (p.5). All examples of 'great art' he cites come from the Euro-American tradition (such as Tolstoy, Mahler, Elgar, Eliot, Shakespeare and Mozart). In arguing for all children's enti-tlement to this highly selective cultural diet, Pascall invokes a deficit model of 'other' cultures, positioning popular cul-ture solely as a tool to help us distinguish between poor art ('a pervasive diet of sloppy speech and soap operas', p.18) and great art. To Pascall, education about the arts is 'part of

a civilising curriculum' which will contribute 'to our moral and spiritual good' (p.11); behind artists such as Mozart or Shakespeare 'lie essential truths about our understanding of humanity' (p.15). Internally contradictory, Pascall's speech exposes his version of the entitlement argument as shallow and excluding. (Coles, 2013b: 37)

Pascall echoes the then Secretary of State for Education, John Patten. At the Tory Party conference in 1992, he proclaimed that, instead of allowing those 'trendy lefty teachers' to destroy 'our great literary heritage', he wanted 'William Shakespeare in our classrooms not Ronald McDonald' (Patten, 1992).

Fast-forward nearly thirty years and Nick Gibb's desire to espouse Hirsch's cultural literacy takes on a different complexion completely. In a speech, significantly entitled 'All pupils will learn our island story', Michael Gove (2010), then the Shadow Secretary of State for Education, speaks of a pupil enraptured by a performance of *Hamlet*, declaring that 'Our literature is the best in the world – it is every child's birthright and we should be proud to teach it in every school.' As the only named author in the English curriculum of 2014, Shakespeare lies at the centre of this claim.

Yet it is not just that the knowledge curriculum, in England at least, has overtly jingoistic tendencies; it is that this knowledge-based, jingoistic curriculum is to be unquestioningly transmitted, to be handed down. Gibb, writing his defence of Hirsch, cites Gove, who says,

> A society in which there is a widespread understanding of the nation's past, a shared appreciation of cultural reference points, a common stock of knowledge on which all can draw, and trade, is a society in which we all understand each other better, one in which the ties that bind are stronger, and more resilient at times of strain … [We should] completely overhaul the curriculum – to ensure that the acquisition of knowledge within rigorous subject disciplines is properly valued and cherished. (Gove, 2009, cited in Gibb, 2015: 13)

The 'shared appreciation', 'cultural reference points' and 'common stock of knowledge' all sound like Hirsch's 'share[d] cultural markers' (Leitch, 2009: 7), which should arise when students all study the same canonical literature. But it is the 'acquisition of knowledge' that makes it sound traditional. John Dewey, the parent of progressive education, defined traditional education as 'prepared forms of skill which comprehend the material instruction' (Dewey, 1935/66: 18). Acquiring knowledge makes it sound as if knowledge is merely handed down, passed on as 'prepared forms of skill'. The sense that knowledge is not something one can get through progressive education is reinforced when Gibb talks of educational practice under a Labour government. He claims, 'To the uninformed outsider, "independent learning", "learning to learn", and "individualised instruction" all sound misleadingly like reasonable ideas. However, reading Hirsch provided me with the mental armour to see these ideas for what they were, and fight them accordingly' (Gibb, 2015: 13). For Gibb, and by implication Hirsch, the thought that pupils could 'learn how to learn' or even learn independently is something he has to do battle with, to clothe himself in 'mental armour' and 'fight'.

As we will see in the later sections, such an approach is very different from the sort advocated by those wanting to adopt a more progressive pedagogy of watching Shakespeare. Yet despite or perhaps because of its opposition to progressive ways of learning, the knowledge curriculum has gained a substantial foothold in England as well as the US. In the States, the influence of Hirsch can be found, for example, in the number of websites dedicated to following his core curriculum. One such is the Core Knowledge site (Core Knowledge, consulted on 24.08.2021), which tells us on its home page that 'E. D. Hirsch Jr. is the founder and chairman of the Core Knowledge Foundation.' The site claims that he has 'as a voice of reason [been] making the case for equality of educational opportunity'. Echoing Tory rhetoric, the home page ends with the dictum that his core knowledge will 'educate our children using common, coherent and sequenced curricula to help heal and preserve the nation', which, up until recently, excluded all that was not white and western European (Yandell, 2017; Marshall, 2020).

In the UK, a number of multi-academy trusts have been set up on the basis that they will teach a knowledge-rich curriculum, all with components on

Shakespeare. So, for example, the Mastery Curriculum (2019) has amongst other plays a unit on *A Midsummer Night's Dream* which starts with a substantial amount of 'factual', so-called historical information before even looking at the text. Robert Eaglestone (2021), a professor of English literature, comments on the SoW, which outlines what it intends the students to acquire: '"The key knowledge: Life in Elizabethan England; life in ancient Athens; Shakespeare's life; the four lovers; the love potion; Elizabethan family relationships", and then only finally, "the form of a play"' (27).

As Eaglestone goes on to point out, 'The historical context is prioritised over how a play works or what a comedy is' (27). The curriculum was originally part of the Ark Academy Trust but is now available as the Mastery Curriculum to purchase for around £6,000. They offer a knowledge-based curriculum in all subjects aimed at pupils aged between eleven and fourteen. Their 'knowledge-rich English curriculum' provides 'teachers with the resources to help students master the ideas, concepts and stories that have shaped the world' (Mastery Curriculum, 2019). The Inspiration Trust (2019) declares that, at the heart of its 'vision', it 'will work with the best educational knowledge – nationally and internationally – in order to create a world-class curriculum'. Others, such as the Pimlico Academy Trust (2019), do not have a published version of their curriculum, but do state 'subjects are taught discretely according to schemes of work that set out what knowledge we expect our students to acquire'.

The use of the word 'acquire' is again significant. Once more it implies that something, in this case knowledge, which students previously lacked, is given, handed down. In this respect the Pimlico Academy owes much to the work of Michael Young. In an article entitled 'Overcoming the Crisis in Curriculum Theory: A Knowledge-Based Approach', he writes in the abstract, 'The paper argues that curriculum theory must begin not from the learner but from the learner's entitlement to knowledge' (Young, 2013). In the paper itself he adds that the 'progressive, learner-centred tradition [which] can be traced back to Rousseau and took its most sophisticated form in writings of those influenced by Dewey' (102) needs to be replaced with 'the question of knowledge' (103). Young is not a Conservative and yet the thrust of his work, which for him is apolitical, sits comfortably within a right-wing agenda.

Robert Eaglestone, again avoiding the political implications of a knowledge-based curriculum, argues vigorously against it for the subject of English. In a pamphlet written as part of a series called Impact, Philosophical Perspectives on Education Policy, Eaglestone (2021) considers the idea that both Hirsch and Young take a scientific approach to knowledge and thus undermine the arts, and in particular English, by forcing them into a scientific model.

For Eaglestone, the subject of English is dialogic in nature. He writes, for example, in an earlier book, *Literature: Why It Matters* (2019), that 'literary studies aims to do something different from most disciplines' (29), adding that while most subjects drive toward consensus, the goal of 'literary studies is to help develop a continuing dissensus [*sic*] about the texts we study' (29–30). Talking of close reading, an activity frequently undertaken at school and university level, he comments that 'Scientists and historians, for example, try and cut down ambiguity, to avoid doubt . . . in close reading the point is to respond to the "simultaneous presence of many meanings" (Wood, 2017, p. 47) rather than draw out one unambiguously . . . "Close reading" then becomes open ended, hard to pin down and shared creative activity' (Wood, 2017, p. 47) (Eagleston, 2019: 45–6).

This is very different from Hirsch's or Young's models (yet similar to the ones we shall examine later when we consider the work of the two teachers). 'Knowledge', Eaglestone (2019) argues, 'is not simply deposited or downloaded but developed in the process of teaching and learning . . . Everything, not simply what is formally stamped as "knowledge", is brought to the experience' (32). In his pamphlet he uses a creative/critical rewriting of *Hamlet* to demonstrate his point. He begins by saying that 'Young's insistence that the focus should be on the knowledge not the knowers may be right for science' but that 'this idea makes the humanities incoherent' (Eaglestone, 2021: 15). He then compares a passage that Young has written on geography to his version of *Hamlet*.

> Pupils' relationships with the 'concept' of a city should be different to their relationship with their 'experience' of London as the city where they live. It is important that the

pupils do not confuse the London that the geography teacher talks about with the London in which they live. To a certain extent, it is the same city, but the pupils' relationship with it in the two cases is not the same. The London where they live is 'a place of experience'. London as an example of a city is 'an object of thought' or a 'concept'. (Young and Lambert, 2014: 98, cited in Eaglestone, 2021: 15)

And then

> Pupils' relationships with the 'concept' of the play *Hamlet* should be different to their relationship with their 'experience' of *Hamlet* as the play they have seen or read. It is important that the pupils do not confuse the *Hamlet* that the English teacher talks about with the *Hamlet* they have experienced. To a certain extent it is the same play, but the pupils' relationship with it in the two cases is not the same. The *Hamlet* they have seen or read is 'a place of experience'. *Hamlet* in the classroom is 'an object of thought' or a 'concept.' (Eaglestone, 2021: 16)

He concludes, 'This division between literature as experience and literature as "classroom object" is just incoherent for English' (16) and, as we shall see, makes little sense when considering the pedagogy of watching Shakespeare. In addition, Young considers knowledge, as he considers science, value free. Yet again, Eaglestone argues, this makes no sense in the study of literature. 'Values are how we orient our discussions of literature: exploring Macbeth's ambition or asking if a character is right to fall in love relies precisely on values and questions about values' (16).

The dismissal of English as a knowledge subject goes back a long way, to the *Newbolt Report* of the Departmental Committee of the Board of Education (1921), and while there are many difficulties with sections of the *Newbolt Report*, the Committee was clear; key to the *Newbolt Report* is the teaching of literature as a 'fine art'. But the Committee goes on to warn,

'The teaching of Literature is beset by many dangers. It is fatal to make it a mere knowledge subject – to concentrate on the getting up of the actual subject matter or school annotations, and equally fatal to substitute for it a mere impression of literary history' (21).

The *Newbolt Report*, then, questions the teaching of English as a 'mere knowledge subject' and criticises 'annotations' and 'a mere impression of literary history', both of which could be said to be characteristic of Hirsch's (1987) 'cultural literacy'. It sits uncomfortably not only with a speech given by Michael Gove lauding the knowledge curriculum, where he wanted '[t]o ensure that the acquisition of knowledge within rigorous subject disciplines is properly valued and cherished' (Gove, 2010, cited in Gibb, 2015: 13), but also with many modern classrooms.

In another passage, the *Newbolt Report* talks of the 'scientific study of the language', adding: 'To give information and insist on its being accurately registered is an almost mechanical manner' (Departmental Committee of the Board of Education, 1921: 11). While the report does not mention memory, it has clear overtones of today's retrieval and rehearsal practices of cognitive load theory (Willingham, 2009; Rosenshine, 2012). For the Committee, such delivery has a 'mechanical manner' which is contrasted with the 'feeling or thought' demanded by good literature teaching (Departmental Committee of the Board of Education, 1921: 11).

The pattern is always the same. If literature becomes a 'mere knowledge subject', then, for example, the teaching of poetry can become 'a mere mechanical drill' (Departmental Committee of the Board of Education, 1921: 111). Teachers can 'harp on the same method lesson after lesson, to read in class minute fragments of a whole . . . To work in successive terms at one and the same book – all these make staleness in class and teacher inevitable' (112). And while they do not want the study of literature to be '[s]entimental . . . The pupils must be aware of literature as the revelation of beauty and the expression of thought and emotion' (117–18). Citing evidence that had been submitted to the Committee, the report claimed that 'Linguistic, historic and comparative methods of dealing with literature in schools have all failed in so far as they have not been tinged with emotion' (118).

Important too, for both the Committee and Eaglestone, is the nature of experience. The Committee writes, for example, that 'the more intelligible and powerful [which] presents the student with experiences of time and circumstances more nearly related to his own' (Departmental Committee of the Board of Education, 1921: 18). Eaglestone, as we have seen, comments, 'Everything, not simply what is formally stamped as "knowledge", is brought to the experience' (Eaglestone, 2019: 32). In fact, in *Literature: Why It Matters*, Eaglestone (2019) takes the example of H_2O and compares it to being caught in a downpour. The 'experience' of the latter – being soaked to the skin – bears no comparison to the knowledge of the former.

The notion of experience, of experiencing, is central to John Dewey's definition of progressive education. He even uses the word in the title of three of his books: *Experience and Education* (1935/1975), *Experience and Nature* (1925) and *Art As Experience* (1934/2005). Interestingly, Michael Young reduces the notion of experience to 'just experience – what we are' (Young and Lambert, 2014: 18). In so doing he dismisses Dewey's use of the word. Yet Dewey's understanding of the word is far richer. In *Democracy and Education*, he writes: 'The nature of experience can be understood only by noting that it includes an active and a passive element peculiarly combined' (Dewey, 1916/2004: 133). In a chapter entitled 'Experience and Thinking', Dewey elaborates. Although he is writing on education generally, rather than English in particular, his words have a disturbing familiarity for English classrooms: 'In schools, those under instruction are too customarily looked upon as acquiring knowledge as theoretical spectators, minds which appropriate knowledge by direct energy of intellect. The very word pupil has almost come to mean one who is engaged not in having fruitful experiences but in absorbing knowledge directly' (Dewey, 1916/2004: 134).

In the opening chapter, 'Education As a Necessity for Life', he links the idea of experience with the idea of dialogue, of communication: '[O]ne has to assimilate, imaginatively, something of another's experience in order to tell him intelligently of one's own experience. All communication is like art . . . Only when it becomes cast in a mould and runs in a routine way does it lose its educative power' (6). It is perhaps significant that he links communication with the imagination and art.

Reader-Response

What is also crucial is that one communicates the internal with the outside, 'an active and a passive element peculiarly combined' (Dewey, 1916/2004: 133). Here Dewey links neatly, though not overtly, with reader-response theories, the dual nature of reading and responding, sometimes to an audience, at others just internal. Reader-response theory became prevalent in English classrooms from the 1970s onwards as a pedagogic way of thinking about a classroom which was student- rather than teacher-centred, and the dialogue that ensues as a result. Although it was not named as such it had peculiar relevance when discussing or writing about diverse classrooms (see, for example, Morgan and Wyatt-Smith, 2000; Marshall, 2003). Again, we will see in the following sections of this Element how reader-response theory resonates with the two teachers, though once more they do not name it.

Yandell (2001), for instance, describes how his views of *Romeo and Juliet* were transformed through an interaction within his classroom with a boy called Michael. Yandell was looking at the line 'What's in a name' and explained how he went on to teach the received, anti-essentialist reading of this speech – who we are should not be dictated by birth. But then Michael intervened. Drawing on the 'popular' culture reference of James Cameron's film *Titanic* and his own experience, he challenged this interpretation of the play. Class, he argues, matters. To ignore it is naïve and, as in the case of both the protagonists of Shakespeare's play and Cameron's film, fatal. Yandell adds, 'What he said made me reconsider the whole speech and its relationship to the rest of the play' (Yandell, 2001: 146). He goes on to write 'I . . . came from Oxford with a smug sense of how much I had to offer. What I found was that I had much to learn. I am embarrassed by the memory of my complacency' (149).

In a more recent publication (Yandell, 2020), this time specifically on reader-response theory, Yandell again writes about a lesson on *Romeo and Juliet*.

> When Monica Brady's Palestinian students study *Romeo and Juliet*, the play's representation of the family, particularly as it is figured in the relationship between Capulet and his daughter, becomes a central focus of inquiry. They want

to know more about the patriarchal character of Renaissance London (or Verona), and they bring what they know of Palestinian family structures to bear on this question. For them, Capulet's decision to marry off Juliet to Paris is an entirely rational response to the effect that Tybalt's death has had in weakening the family's position. At the same time, the space to explore the play is also a space to examine the operation of patriarchal structures and assumptions within the society of Ramallah (Brady, 2015; Yandell & Brady, 2016). In this approach, neither the context of a text's production nor that of its reception can be regarded as a given: the prism of the literary text allows both to become problematised objects of renewed scrutiny. (28)

Yandell reveals how the response of the readers differs from that of the teacher and a dialogue takes place in which a new understanding emerges for the reading of the play. Bridget Escolme, in her book *Talking to the Audience: Shakespeare, Performance, Self*, observes that 'It is, perhaps, the range of ways in which Shakespeare's plays produce a role for the spectator in the production of meaning that has allowed countless subsequent writers and theatre practitioners to claim that his concerns are identical to those of their own historical period' (Escolme, 2005: 20). But it also gives scope for students within a class to fathom their own readings of the play and in so doing transform the views of others.

In her book *Theatre Audiences* Susan Bennett (2005 (1997)) was amongst the first to relate reader-response theory to the role of the spectator. She writes, 'I have started with the work of these and other reception-orientated theorists as many of their ideas applied in some way to the particular structures of theatre, and as their vocabulary has been helpful in finding my own model for audience' (45). She goes on to give a brief history of reader-response theorists, starting with Norman Holland and working her way through Stanley Fish, Wolfgang Iser and Hans Robert Jauss amongst others, pointing out their strengths and weaknesses. Citing Jauss, for instance, she comments, as we have just seen in Monica Brady's class, that he felt that 'Literary works are measured not only against works, but against the readers' social experience' Benett, 2005 (1997): 80. And again, quoting Jauss, she explores the notion of intertextuality, a merging of the contemporary with historic, as we saw with Michael's reading of *Romeo and Juliet*. 'It brings to light the history of a text's reception and dispels the notion of objective and timeless meaning contained independently within a text. Because of this, we can learn about an unknown work by measuring it against its intertexts (implicitly or explicitly cited' (90).

She also considers the way that Jauss' theory of interpretive communities can be seen in the reception of Harold Pinter's *The Birthday Party*. Its first run lasted only a few performances as it was poorly reviewed. But it came back a few years later to rapturous acclaim by the critics. Bennett considers too the work of Iser, whose reader-response theory is more politicised.

Iser sets up a three-way approach to the analysis of reading: consideration of the text, of the reader, and, most importantly, the conditions of interaction between the two. At the centre is the concept of the implied reader which 'offers a means of describing the process whereby textual structures are transmuted through ideational activities into personal experiences' (Iser, 1978: 38). Yet Iser's real interest is the text itself (Bennett (2005 (1997): 80).

Again, the notion of a reader's experience is highlighted. What is interesting about Bennett's brief history of reader-response theory is that she does not mention Louise Rosenblatt, who is frequently cited among teacher practitioners. Her first book, *Literature and Exploration*, was actually written in 1938, well before the theorists Bennett refers to, and is a lone female voice amongst so many men. Her central message was that readers give meaning to the texts they read (as we shall see in the following sections). Patricia Harkin (2005) and Yandell (2020) both argue that the demise of reader-response theory has come about through its becoming mainstream; the role of the reader's response has become too obvious to be worth noting. Nevertheless, writing for the National Council of Teachers of English, Harkin commented that,

> Iser's and Rosenblatt's emphasis on the transactional character of reading were particularly popular because they offered critics and teachers a chance to have it both ways.

On the one hand, they allowed practitioners to retain the common-sense notions that authors intend something when they write and that readers do tend to behave as though they were the recipients of a message that they should do their best to understand. On the other, they could simultaneously hold the equally common-sensical notion that authorial intention is unknowable and that constructed meanings are disparate and contextualised. (Harkin, 2005: 412–13)

For Harkin,

Rosenblatt's distinction between efferent and esthetic readings provides both students and teachers a useful way of discriminating kinds of reading activities: sometimes we read simply to obtain information (How are the Cubs doing?) while at other times we read for the pleasurable experience of generating interpretations (Is Robert Frost dealing with metaphysical uncertainty in 'After Apple-Picking' or is he just talking about picking apples?) Rosenblatt pointed out that these different purposes call for differing strategies. (412)

Here in the distinction between efferent and esthetic readings can also be seen the distinction between mechanical and emotional readings. We could see it also as reading that is completed from a knowledge-rich curriculum and one that is experiential. For Eaglestone it might be reading which is scientific, the text as a mere vehicle of information, and one which is arts based, 'generating interpretations'. The difficulty in a climate where the curriculum is knowledge-based is that all reading can become efferent of a kind, omitting the reader's response.

Spectator Theory

Harkin goes on to speak of the 'transactional character' of a text or play (412) and observes that 'authorial intention is unknowable' (413). In so doing we discover that the notion of reader response elides neatly with spectator theory.

Spectator theory, amongst other things, emphasises the significance of audience (or spectator) responses to a performance as opposed to arriving at a definitive understanding of a play/text. In her book *Shakespeare, Spectatorship and the Technologies of Performance*, Pascale Aebischer (2020) also includes the performer when writing about the role of the audience watching a performance. So she speaks of 'theatre's capacity to endow both actor and spectator with the ability to respond, to contribute to the production of images and to bring their own personal experience into play' (6–7). For Aebischer this sets up a kind of 'triangulation' (8) between audience/spectator, performer and production of the play in creating meaning, and this idea is foregrounded.

As Bennett, concluding her survey of reader-response theory, quotes Mary Louise Pratt,

> Reader-response criticism and pedagogy clearly capitalize on the culture's intense focus on self-knowledge and self-observation, and on the validity now accorded to personal and intuitive knowledge. Students come to us trained, like ourselves, in observing their own responses, in talking about them, and in considering them important . . . this is an improvement over formalism, if only because it is true, among other things, that readers make meaning. (Pratt, 1986; cited in Benett, 2005 (1997): 35

Bennett transfers this to spectator theory and we shall see examples, in Sections 1 and 2, how students 'in observing their own responses, in talking about them, and in considering them important' create meanings for themselves. Bridget Escolme, for instance, 'acknowledge[s] that performance conventions produce meaning, and to explore the meanings that a convention used in the past might produce today, is to avoid that naivety' (Escolme, 2005: 17) She adds later that she is 'going to speculate as to how far the meaning produced by the shifting distance between performer and audience might be constitutive of the ways in which the plays produce meaning' (19). Indeed, part of the purpose of her book is to explore ways in which the characters on stage 'conspire with us, plead with us, confront us, bully us, vow to please us, and I want to argue that the unpredictability of our reactions – the multiplicity of our readings, the uncertainness of our pleasure and support – are integral to the readings that the plays make possible' (19).

The Pedagogy of Watching Shakespeare

And it is here that we start to think about the pedagogy of watching Shakespeare in schools. The following sections, as noted, are written by serving teachers. They are different in style. Myfanwy Edwards' section arises out of research-based, focus group discussion but the kind of dialogue it involves could just as easily be a part of any post-production lesson where students have the chance to comment on what they have seen. Although her work is not based in a particular school, the practice of taking students to see a play they are studying is commonplace. In addition, the National Theatre now has a large digital platform, the National Theatre Live, that gives free access to schools to watch a large number of their productions (see Aebischer, 2019; Bennett, 2019). There are also, of course, countless film versions of plays, particularly of Shakespeare).

Section 2 looks at how Charlotte Dixey writes and then adapts an SoW for students studying for their A-level exams taken when they are eighteen years old. It is a narrative account, punctuated by comments from students and other teachers in her department, about teaching *Hamlet*. She cites some revisions that happen: how, for example, she decided to teach a lesson on varieties of interpretation of the play at the start of the SoW rather than at the end (Semenza, 2003). She uses clips from the Olivier (1948), Branagh (1996), Icke and Huw (2017), Zeffirelli (1990) and Doran (2009) adaptations to help the students see how film directors vary in their understandings of the play.

Both Myfanwy Edwards and Charlotte Dixey show at a practical level how watching Shakespeare enhances students' understanding of his work. And moreover, it lends, as we shall see, new insight into his plays. In Charlotte Dixey's section, she argues that watching a selection of Shakespearean adaptations can elicit a richer audience/reader response from students. By teaching students to evaluate performance, they intuitively hone their own critical voices and authority becoming both active spectator and active critic themselves.

2 Identity and Watching the National Theatre's School's *Macbeth* Directed by Justin Audibert (2017)

This section focuses on excerpts from post-show discussions with young audiences who had watched the National Theatre's touring production of *Macbeth* for schools (NT, 2017; director Justin Audibert). The students involved attended Birnam, Cawdor, Glamis and Dunsinane schools and were in Years 10–13 in 2017.[1] I was fortunate in my research to have the support of Jane Ball, who was then the director of secondary and further education at The National Theatre. I did not receive any funding from the Theatre and all contact I made with schools was done independently, but Jane was enthusiastic about my project and enabled me to access the production and the team. I was invited to rehearsals and was able to interview her before the tour began in November 2016 and during the tour in March 2017. The tour comprised two mountings of the production with individual actors playing multiple parts. Nana Amoo-Gottfried played Macbeth in both mountings. Another consistency was that the cast members were ethnically diverse, with only one White actor in either mounting. Both productions switched the gender of key characters: in the first Banquo was played by a woman whilst in the second it was Macduff who was played by a woman. The play was set in a post-apocalyptic Scotland in a non-specific timeline. Lucy Sierra's production design took inspiration from steam-punk. The costumes were steam-punk in style, including witches in gas masks leering over toxic waste cauldrons. The set comprised a black mat and a 'scaffold' behind which characters could hide/change and upon which they could climb or sit. These choices were discussed enthusiastically by the young people in my focus groups and frequently queried in the Q&As the tour held after school performances.

---

[1] In the UK school Years 10–13 represent students aged between fourteen and eighteen.

In the conversations I draw upon for this section the young people respond to the casting of the play, particularly in relation to the gender and race of the actors. I hope that through this short introduction to some of what they say, we, as teachers and as theatre practitioners, might begin to pay more attention to how we frame productions for young people and what young people have to say in response to them. The conversations I had with the young people show the multiplicity of voices, experiences and feelings present in a theatre audience. The discussions reveal the way in which casting and staging impact not only participants' responses to the play and the production but also their sense of themselves and their relationship with *Macbeth* as a text. The complexity of the responses to the casting and the music shows us the knowledge and understanding of identity young people bring with them to a performance. More than this, the conversations reveal the ideas they were provoked into exploring through not only watching the play but also during the opportunity to discuss it with their peers.

Central to my argument is the idea that the performance of race, gender and to a certain extent in this context, class, as with all theatre, is reliant on the audience; the way that race, class, and gender are enacted within their own communities or cultural worlds is central to their relevance to the production. The questions and ideas these young people raised in the time I spent with them cannot be done justice to here. Even if I did have more space to explore the interviews, the 'multiple contingencies of subjective response, context and environment which condition an individual's interpretation of a particular performance event' could never be fully available to me as a researcher (Freshwater, 2009: 5–6). I am wary too of filtering 'their heterogeneous voices through [my] own voice' especially as a White, heterosexual woman and in the position of researcher and teacher (Thompson, 2017: 3). Those identities inevitably come into play when thinking about what the participants said to me and how I then read their responses.

'Black Macbeth'

When Ayanna Thompson (2011) wrote about Shakespeare and race in 2011, she stated that we ought not to consider whether race impacts audience reception but that we should assume it does and consider how that impact manifests. This section will be framed by that assumption and will seek to show the ways in which the impact of a racially diverse cast is manifest within the bounds of the research. She argues too that 'color-blind' casting upholds a kind of 'historical amnesia' where race is of little to no significance (27). She develops this in her later work, stating that even 'when race is mentioned in most contemporary reception scholarship, it is a passing nod to the fact that both the cast's and the audience's diversity may impact reception' rather than an exploration of that impact (5). Just as her edited collection *The Cambridge Companion to Shakespeare and Race* seeks to 'challenge the supposed neutrality of a color-blind approach to teaching, reading, and/or performing Shakespeare' (Thompson, 2021: 11), I want to show that the National Theatre's casting choices were by no means 'blind' and to consider the work Black actors were being asked to do symbolically on top of performing Shakespeare to a high standard. Furthermore, I want to show how important that work was to the audiences who were predominantly school students.

As part of her role Jane Ball frequently reaches out to teachers to gather their opinions on projects in development. Having expressed an interest in the idea of a touring production, I met with Jane to talk about what the theatre were hoping to do when the tour was in its earliest stages. Part of the conversation I had with Jane regarded the casting and her opinions on it. We were both sceptical about a female Banquo, but we did not question the colour-blind casting. In March 2017, when the production had been touring for a few months, I interviewed her more formally about the development of the production and once again we turned to the cast.

Jane: But what I would say more so than with, if we just had Macbeth with a famous person in the Olivier [theatre] then you would come to that as a school and you know the kids would get a lot out of it, but it wouldn't have been created with an audience of teenagers in mind.

And, part of also what we're doing, and it was interesting going into the schools in Eastleigh was that, like we're doing it with a really diverse cast and a teacher said to one of the actors there, the guy playing Macbeth, and she said to him 'these boys' and they were all non-White boys, 'would never imagine that Macbeth would be anything like them and that seeing you playing this character, and actually they can relate to it a lot more and their experience of studying the play will be different because they'll now not imagine Macbeth as a middle aged white man.

Here it appears that not only is Amoo-Gottfreid seen to be taking on the title role of *Macbeth*, but he is also viewed as a reflection of and role model to young Black men in the audience both by being on stage and by playing the protagonist of the play. In the anecdote about the teacher and 'these boys,' it is Amoo-Gottfried who is spoken to, but it is important to note that in the whole production there is only one White actor. The Black bodies on the stage perform race both within and outside the play-world. The way in which the bodies of Black actors are read, specifically here but also, as Young suggests, more widely, is intertwined entirely with skin colour in a way that White actors playing these roles rarely if ever experience. This 'complected' moment or 'charged, racialized and racializing scenario' (Young, 2010: 10–11) evidences the frequent tension between the physical Black body (of an individual) versus the conceptual (created from 'largely imagined' aspects being 'located within' a physical body) (7). Both Jane and the teacher are clearly suggesting it is a positive thing that the cast is diverse (the conceptual) and yet in doing so they place a burden on Amoo-Gottfried's performance (as an individual Black body).

Jane mentions that Amoo-Gottfried is in a concurrent production – also part of the tour – *Romeo and Juliet* (director Beijan Sheibani, 2016). In both productions, Audibert chose to use different models of non-traditional Shakespearean casting, but the same actors. *Romeo and Juliet* uses a controversial form of the 'cross cultural' casting model where the delineation of rival groups is done on racial lines within a production.

> particularly because we're going to schools in London and you know schools in London tend to have a more diverse student population. And because they had to be dual cast with Romeo and Juliet as well which is a remount of that production so it's already been done twice before and it's an Asian and African, like the two families so that they needed to reflect that.

In *Romeo and Juliet*, the way they have transposed the action to a 'vivid urban backdrop' (National Theatre, 2016) deliberately emphasises the racial differences of the cast to one another. *Macbeth*, on the other hand, ostensibly uses a 'societal' casting model. In the societal casting model, the non-White actors are cast in roles that reflect the contemporary societal norms of the production's context so that no statement is made by their casting nor is any attention drawn to their 'otherness' (Thompson, 2011: 8). As Jane points out, the 'society' into which this production is placed – that of London schools – does mean that the casting reflects societal norms to a degree. However, the director, Justin Audibert, transposed the action to an undefined, post-apocalyptic future. During Q&A at the end of several performances, the cast explained that this setting allowed them to use non-traditional casting because they did not have to play by contemporary society's hierarchical rules. One way of looking at this decision is to say that by using this as a justification for non-traditional casting, Audibert tells the audience that societal casting would not work if the play were set even in a contemporary world because it might not allow for a young Black king or for Black women as warriors. As with so much dystopia, Audibert's vision, to the young people watching, bore resemblance to their world in important ways, despite attempting to distance itself from it. On the other hand, by transposing the action, Audibert arguably attempts to avoid what Harvey Young describes as the point at which 'the individual becomes anonymously or, more accurately, metonymically Black' (Young, 2010: 7) rather than being seen as a distinct person or character. By moving the action away from the contemporary world and away from either Shakespeare's England or medieval Scotland, Audibert attempts to allow Black actors the freedom to play roles in which they are not traditionally cast (Chakravarty, 2021: 190–207) without the imposition of contemporary symbolism.

Road Man

One of the issues raised in the growing body of work on race and Shakespearean casting is the existence and desirability of a post-racial society. Young describes something called '[c]ritical memory . . . the act of reflecting upon and sharing recollections of embodied black experience [which] assists the process of identifying connections across black bodies and acknowledges that related histories of discrimination, violence, and migration result in similar experiences' (Young, 2010: 18). For the young audiences I spoke to, there is a clear sense of this. Rather than living in a society where race is irrelevant, they share critical memory that allows them to identify and relate to action on stage in a way that is possible specifically because of the perceived race of the actors. This idea comes through quite clearly in the section of dialogue taken from the post-show discussion at Glamis.

Bella:	Because like, in the movie um what's the guy that was trying to be rude? The killer! In the movie he was like sophisticated and stuff but in the play he made it a bit more like what we'd see us, so it's kind of like we can see like another aspect to it.
Vaughn:	He was the funniest guy.
Me:	Did you like that they did that?
Bella:	Yeah....
Me:	So you talked about the roadman. Firstly, 'cause I do know what you mean, but can one of you specifically tell me what you mean? Bella you brought it up. When you say he was being a roadman, what exactly do you mean?
Bella:	Like streetwise.
Aki:	The way he spoke.
Bella:	He was like walking and talking like.
Aki:	He spoke like us.
JJ:	It was very informal.
Me:	So do you mean like his tone? And like?
Vince:	And also that finger point thing he did poking the guy in the chest.
JJ:	His hand expressions were different.
Bella:	He was doing like guns.
JJ:	[Laughing] Yeah.
Bella:	I was so confused.

Within this excerpt the group from Glamis are discussing the portrayal of the Murderer in the play. This production, due to a small cast, had one Murderer in the violent scenes rather than three. The dialogue was not modernised. Ashley Gerlack, who played the Murderer, was asked about his portrayal more than once in the Q&A sessions after the performances. In his answer he explained that he wanted to make sure the character was distinctive because he was playing several parts and so he drew on the Grime music he loves in the creation of the Murderer.[2] From the conversation just cited, his rendering was clearly successful. His use of gesture – 'finger guns' – and accent or perhaps intonation – 'the way he spoke' – are noted and the overall effect suggested he was 'streetwise', 'rude' and, earlier in the conversation, a 'roadman'.

The terms used to describe the character are racialised. In West London, where Glamis is situated, the descriptor 'rude' or 'roadman' is used fairly ubiquitously to describe all kinds of people. However, more usually, 'for the millennial male of colour, the title "roadman" is somewhere between an accusation and an accolade, a perversely aspirational archetype that offers status from the margins' (Boakye, 2019: 357). A simple definition is 'a man who lives on and by the rules of the road'. deriving from Grime culture and the Caribbean-derived 'rudeboy' archetype (357). That tension between accusation and accolade is seen in the discussion. Aki and Bella respectively point out the way the 'killer' 'spoke like us' and reflected 'the way we see us'. When Bella contrasts Gerlack's performance with the same character 'in the movie' she is recalling Michael Balfour's performance ('he was like sophisticated and stuff') of the First Murderer in Roman Polanski's *Macbeth* (1971). In this case it seems that the character being relatable to them is more important than sophistication, indeed sophistication is presented as alienating. However, there is also light mockery in what they say. The recognition of an actor borrowing the 'finger guns' and the way of 'walking and talking' common to them was funny. Through the phrase 'trying to be rude' we get the sense that they appreciate his attempt but that he has fallen short.

Gerlack's decision to portray the character in this way draws attention to the class status of the Murderer within the play-world. Despite the actors and director claiming that in the post-apocalyptic setting the normal hierarchies do not apply, Gerlack decided to depict the Murderer in a way

[2] 'Grime is a genre of electronic music that emerged in London in the early 2000s. It developed out of the earlier UK dance style UK garage, and draws influences from jungle, dancehall, and hip hop' (*Wikipedia* consulted on 30 September 22).

that specifically ties him to Black, working-class, immigrant culture. Some of the mockery of the archetype from the group potentially comes from the same place derision of this archetype comes from in the real world: snobbery, racism and classism. Though the students in this group come from a background where they would encounter this archetype regularly and perhaps be cast in the role themselves (as they say he was portraying the Murderer 'the way we see us'), the term 'roadman' is quite often used as an insult. The description of the character as a roadman could suggest that they see the Murderer, as portrayed by Gerlack, as a loser rather than as someone who has mastered the streets. Whether or not this is what Gerlack intended, there is certainly a powerful link between this tension and the world Shakespeare was attempting to convey. Macbeth is perhaps a king lowering himself by consorting with ignoble thugs but they can do things he is too cowardly to do himself and he knows that their desire to avenge their own honour is strong. Or perhaps this is a reflection of the fluidity of power relations in the new world order created by Macbeth's actions.

The way the Glamis group talks about Gerlack's performance in some detail shows how much it stood out to them. It also shows how well Gerlack performed a now archetypal Black identity. I do not know the extent to which Gerlack is immersed in the Grime culture he consumes, but Grime music has made a specifically British, urban, predominantly Black, male identity culturally mainstream. The finger guns and poking a guy in the chest are easily replicable but a way of walking is harder to convincingly emulate. Gerlack's own Blackness and the fact that the characters he engages with in role were also played by Black men and women heighten how recognisable these gestural tropes are and how close to reality they appear to the young, ethnically diverse, London-based audience watching them.

The effect of this decision is echoed in my interview with students from Cawdor. This time the focus was on the character of Macbeth being played by a Black actor (Nana Amoo-Gottfried). Jay, asked what he thought of the play, said: Jay: What I liked about it was erm?? Changed the characters. For example when I read the play I thought Macbeth was a white Macbeth I thought it was going to be all English and they changed it. They made it a Black Macbeth it was different to what I expected.

Although this is a small section of the conversation, it is very revealing. 'English' is here contrasted with Blackness. In both these conversations Blackness is contrasted not to Whiteness explicitly but to things which the young people see as different to themselves: Englishness and sophistication. We see a construction of Whiteness within their words but a complex one that is tied up in feelings of national identity/affiliation and class. These young people feel included in a production that attempted to represent their worlds by not only casting Black actors, but also attempting to make the play Black. The action seemed to them to be situated in a recognisable world rather than one in which they were outsiders.

Carol Mejia LaPerle (2021) points out that in an increasingly globalised Early Modern context, the 'fair/dark binary' in Shakespeare's tragedies represents the 'border formations between White Englishness and the blackened other – a conceptual border that dramatic stagings mobilize and complicate' (90). Yet we see that same border being formed in these interviews conducted in 2017. LaPerle's argument is that the genre of tragedy's 'investments in defining civility, legitimacy, and morality are profoundly intertwined with modes of racialization'. Although *Macbeth* is not a focus of LaPerle's essay, the binary between 'White Englishness and the blackened other' is clear in *Macbeth*. Part of the resolution of the play is the replacement of Macbeth the 'butcher' (*Macbeth* V, viii, 69) with Malcom, who is 'compass'd with thy Kingdom's pearl.' He represents a new era for Scotland as an ally of England where 'the most pious Edward' is king (*Macbeth* III, vi, 27). LaPerle aligns moral purity with early modern constructions of race. Combining his presentation as pure with his legitimate bloodline and the image of him enshrined within a pearl symbolises not only the link between moral purity and precious, natural whiteness, but also Englishness (the pearl we see repeated as an image very clearly racialised in *Othello*). Rather than, as in Shakespeare's *Henry V*, the Scottish and English are seen as racially incompatible, in *Macbeth* the relationship between the two is legitimate, purifying and strengthening. Malcolm's kingdom rids the Scots of the 'black' (*Macbeth*, IV, iii, 51) and corrupted tyranny they were under, remains Scottish, welcomes those hidden in Ireland back and joins forces with England, reminding us that 'concepts of race, nation and blood were intertwined' (Hadfield, 2021: 64).

Built into the play, then, is an understanding of Englishness as White and blackness as other to that. Yet there is not, as in some of the other plays (for example, Othello's speech before he dies), anything in the story that allows the othered to speak back. Because in this play there are no characters who are racialised as Black, the black as evil within the play-world cannot be challenged. Perhaps though, through the casting of all the characters with actors of Black and South Asian heritage, the production does, to some degree, problematise the binary. Characters meant to represent the legitimate blood lines, morality and piety are not racially delineated from those who are demonic, magical, 'fiend like' and murderous (*Macbeth*, V, vi, 69). Despite this, in Shakespeare's work and almost certainly his stage and those of his contemporaries, being physically black/ened would have aligned one with darkness, immorality or impurity in some sense. Yet it is still, perhaps, arguable that this is a successful production that works both 'with and against the industry that is Shakespeare', using casting as a strategy (Grier, 2021: 238).

The conversation with the students from Glamis highlights the perceived difference between the students and the 'industry that is Shakespeare' (Grier, 2021: 238). They use the collective pronouns 'we' and 'us' to explain how they felt about the casting. When they use these terms, they are not including me – someone they see, I think, as part of the industry of Shakespeare and of education. As can be seen in the transcript, I wanted to allow them to do this and to explain things that I do understand on some level but am not a part of. In the interview just cited, Jane Ball comments that the National Theatre wanted the production to clearly be made 'with an audience of teenagers in mind', and for the casting to reflect the diversity of London schools. She sets the production apart by linking the diversity of the casting with the choice of performance space and the relatively unknown cast when she says that they could have 'just had Macbeth with a famous person in the Olivier [theatre]'. The Olivier and famous actors represent the English or 'National' way Shakespeare has been and continues to be framed. Jane doesn't suggest that this version of Shakespeare is no good for school audiences, but she does emphasise a desire to make this production one that is differentiated from it. Sometime after having this conversation with Jane, the production for schools was taken off the National Theatre stage because Rufus Norris, who had recently been made artistic director of the National Theatre, decided to produce *Macbeth* on the Olivier stage with Rory Kinnear as Macbeth. Not wanting two productions of the same play on at the theatre, the Macbeth for Schools closed. Through this decision, Norris pushed a production already marginalised out of his Theatre. The border between 'White Englishness and the blackened other' was solidified (238).

There is something to be said here about the language of Shakespeare being combined with the language and signs of modernity and with the racialised language suggested by the performance of the Murderer. Given our educational context, we might usefully consider the way Shakespeare is sometimes considered a cultural shibboleth, theoretically allowing marginalised groups to be a part of a White British cultural identity from which they are implicitly and sometimes explicitly excluded (see this concept explored in more detail in Section 1 of this Element). Whilst Gerlack is speaking nothing but the lines of Shakespeare, he is racialised by the young people watching the play. They do this in a way that he has designed himself but that is only possible because in his role as Murderer he is racialised as Black and therefore his speech and gestures can be read in a way that he says was supposed to be associated with Grime music. The language used is written by the ultimate sign of English cultural supremacy – Shakespeare himself – and yet still the speaker is looked at as a young Black man engaging in the performance of the masculine archetype of 'roadman' or 'rude boy'.

In looking at English language learners, Flores and Rosa note a similar phenomenon. They look at standardised or 'appropriateness' based language practices that seek to bring language learners' speech into a standard form deeming, for example, Black American English as inappropriate. They argue that 'additive' approaches to language teaching that suggest a model of 'appropriateness' fall short in two ways: because no matter the language used the perception of the listener will always racialise the person speaking and also because it does nothing to address the marginalisation of home languages and the notion of being linguistically 'deviant' (Flores and Rosa, 2015: 150). On Twitter and then interviewed in *Spiked* Katherine Birbalsingh, the chair of the Social Mobility Commission for the Conservative Government in the UK, has explicitly cited Grime music, and Stormzy in particular, as dangerous to young people's education (O'Neill, 22 December 21). Therefore, in the UK's educational context, Gerlack's performance does, to some extent, appear to address the marginalisation of the 'deviant' language of Grime by basing a performance of a Shakespearean character on its linguistic and gestural tropes flying in the face of Birbalsingh's fears that Stormzy might be dangerous to young minds.

Though Toni Morrison (1993) argues that regardless of the race of the author, readers are always racialised as White (which is also how Flores and Rosa see the implied listener in their research), it is perhaps fair to say that for this particular production, the audience or readers were not presumed to be all White (xii). Indeed, quite opposite assumptions were made about the ethnic makeup of the audiences based on their youth and urban situation that informed the diversity of casting. What this means, though, is that, perhaps, rather than seeing the audience's racialised discussion of the Murderer as entirely problematic, we might see this production as intentionally and successfully linguistically heteroglossic. When students who identified as feeling an affinity with the presentation of the Murderer discussed it, they emphasised that connection through their own use of language. They communicated their ideas about Shakespeare in 'a language that was valid and necessary at home, in school and in the [streets]' (Baker-Bell, 2020: 4).[3] Through the use of their own language they were able to take ownership of this version of Shakespeare, thereby differentiating between this production and the 'sophisticated' Shakespeare of Michael Balfour they were expecting. The use of their dialect and colloquialisms when describing Gerlack's performance is a shared acknowledgement of collective identity.

Of course, whilst Bella sees the portrayal of the Murderer as 'how we'd see us' not all of the young people in the audience felt the same way. When the students I interviewed at Birnam, a school in North London, discussed

---

[3] Baker-Bell uses the word 'hood' in her text, but she is explicitly talking about American language and I think that, based on my students' use of language and Boakye's explanation of it, 'street' is a culturally appropriate alternative here (Boakye, 2019: 360).

the play, the scene with the Murderer came up once more. This time the reaction was slightly different:

> Amelia: The thing that I thought was weird was the comic relief of the first Murderer because like the murder is such like an important part like the fact that this is Mac, not just Macbeth killing like someone who's like higher than him but killing like and equal killing, like his friend in order to get above, like, that's one of the ultimate betrayals I think. It's like friendship where you view each other as equals rather than like your superior. So then the fact that they made that scene kind of comical.

Me:	Do you think that was intentional?
Amelia:	What? Making it seem comical?
Me:	Yeah, making it comical. Do you think the actor—
Fergal:	Yeah, it was.
Amelia:	I think if you . . . I think it's just so different from all the other characters in the play that it kind of—
Chloe:	It was a contrast to Shakespeare which is quite metaphorical and like doesn't literally say it like it's not like 'I'm gonna kill you' there will be a whole speech, whereas the first Murderer that what it literally was what he said which was . . . (?)

Chloe makes the assumption that Gerlack's lines have been altered from Shakespeare's to create a comic effect in contrast to a more complex and 'metaphorical' 'whole speech'. In the conversation there is no recognition of the cultural references or lifestyle on which Gerlack is drawing. His performance is seen as at odds with the rest of the play and comedic. This section of the interview is important because it emphasises the subjectivity of audience interpretation of both plays in performance and in reading. For Chloe the emphasis on the Murderer's lower class and stark contrast to Macbeth's nobility took away from the depth of feeling she felt ought to occur in the moment the audience sees Macbeth betray Banquo. Chloe does not actively racialise the portrayal of the Murderer. In fact, because of the casting, it is arguably more the performance of class that Chloe is objecting to. That Gerlack would make the Murderer ridiculous is her problem. Yet as we have seen, to another group of students, what Chloe sees as ridiculous can be seen as a fairly realistic, if slightly incongruous, portrayal of a young Black, masculine Londoner. For Jay at Cawdor there was no comedy in the play, only 'betrayal and conflict and stuff that happens in today's society', portrayed by 'a Black Macbeth'. For the students at Glamis a streetwise 'roadman', comedic though he might be to an extent, worked as a way of creating a relatable world in which to set the action. Amelia and Chloe's interpretation jars with the intentions Jane Ball set out to make the play reflective of the young people of London. Similarly to what Bella says, though with a very different perspective, Amelia and Chloe feel that Gerlack's portrayal lacks sophistication.

In one sense the contrasting reactions suggest that the issues faced by Black actors performing Shakespeare are writ large here. You have an ethnically diverse group of young people, all of whom nod along and agree with Bella when she says that this character reflects their lives and Jay, a young Black man pleasantly surprised to see that Shakespeare's characters can be Black. On the other hand, you have a group of White students at Birnam who find the use of street language funny and problematic but enjoy the performances of the Black actors on stage who do not, as explicitly as Gerlack, deviate from more traditional portrayals of the characters. They make assumptions that because of the very things that JJ, Bella and Aki recognised as 'rude', Gerlack must have edited the dialogue because Shakespeare wouldn't have written something like that. We might read into this that the language – in all senses of that word – of the home or the street is not welcome in the performance of Shakespeare. We might also read this as suggesting that performances of 'Black Macbeth' will speak only to Black audiences.

There are, however, other ways of interpreting what is going on here. There is work to be done so students like Chloe might be able to see what Gerlack was doing with that part. However, there is also evidence here of the multiplicity of justified responses to a Shakespearean performance made possible by attempting to reflect the diversity of urban England in the casting of a Shakespeare play. Both responses were affective to some degree. Both were about how the performance made them feel. Both Chloe and Jay compare their expectations of what they were going to see with the reality. Whilst this analysis has considered Gerlack's performance as racialised, it is important to acknowledge that Chloe does not consciously do this herself and that her response is based on a feeling that Macbeth's betrayal of Banquo is let down in a moment that focused the audience's attention on the Murderer. I mention class here too because it should be noted that Bella is of Hispanic descent and her relationship with race, though not the focus of this section, is possibly complex. It is not fair to directly contrast the reactions of Bella and Chloe only through the lens of race. From what they say in the conversations, it is clear that Bella and Chloe position themselves very differently in relation to the 'rude' or 'roadman' character.

It Was Cool; It Was a Cool Thing to Look At

Turning away from the London-based students to those from the north of England at Dunsinane, the responses to the 'mixed race cast' were very positive in the interview group, but this positivity came from quite a different angle. I will return to the discussion of gender and sexuality, but it's important to have the context of the comments about the race of the cast here for analysis:

Amy: And a completely mixed raced cast because it's something that you don't see and, we you know, in 2017 LGBT community all this like 'there's no minorities any more, everyone is equal' [a few voices agree with her as she speaks] it's crazy to think that the same sex couples in Macbeth would be so, d'you know what I mean, alien to us, and yet I mean, there's people here that are homosexual, and that's not a thing, nobody's bothered, and to see it in that and be acted with, and everyone runs with it it's, I think it's interesting. I know, I suppose you could, like, include that in transposing it but it was just it was cool; it was a cool thing to look at.

Like Jay from Cawdor School, Amy is pleased and surprised to see that 'people here' are represented in ways they had not seen before on the stage. Amy is a sixth-form student who is keen to study drama and theatre. Moreover, they have been shown other productions over the years because their school is part of an arts scheme. Her comments about how rare the cross gender and 'mixed race' casting is in 2017 are comments made from anecdotal but, considering her age, fairly extensive experience thanks to the arts programmes and her own enthusiasm for theatre. To compound her point, after the show had finished and I was hovering close to the stage waiting for my group to arrive, another girl came up to me. She was nervous and wanted to ask a question. What she asked was whether there was a meaning behind the non-White cast. She wanted to know if it was significant in some way. Though the school had students from a range of ethnic backgrounds, the whole area and the school is predominantly White and working class. She had never seen a play where all the actors were non-White. Because of her experiences and possibly her surroundings, she saw the Black actors not 'how we'd see us' like Bella, but as probably symbolic in some way. Whilst Amy felt that UK theatre is clearly not keeping up with the accepting, minority-less society, the question the anonymous girl posed suggests that perhaps it does not seem as obvious to everyone that what they saw on stage was a reflection of normality.

Twice in the transcript the 'mixed race' casting is mentioned alongside the acknowledgement of same-sex couples in the play.

Hope: I just were gonna say about like the same sex couple thing and it was it was just nice to see when, and the mix race thing it was like [pause] I think like, especially with Shakespeare and plays, you sort of put up a barrier.

Both times, there is little remark about the fact that the actors are Black other than that it is 'nice to see' and to 'look at'. Much more is said about the impact of the gender switching. There is in this group a clear desire to emphasise that they thought having a 'mixed race' cast was a way of ensuring that groups usually marginalised were represented. However, the students themselves, all being White and coming from an area that was predominantly so, who have classmates they know to be LGBTQ+, feel more able to discuss the impact of the gender switching. Unlike the students from inner London who recognise nuanced verbal and gestural codes embedded in the Black performance of the Murderer, here the students do not see much beyond the complexion of the actors, though they do seem aware that there are people who would be able to do that.

Their conflation of LGBTQ+ identity with racial identity, when considered with Amy's comment that 'there's no more minorities anymore', might tell us that the students here are naïve in their understanding of issues of identity and representation. Yet there is a willingness to celebrate the National Theatre's attempt to be inclusive that is hopeful and not to be dismissed.

Yeah, Irish

In the final part of this section, I want to touch on the White, Irish racial identity that is very subtly brought into the production. One of the student participants, Clodagh, is an Irish student. We open the conversation at Dunsinane with me asking everyone their names so as to make my transcriptions easier. When Clodagh gives hers, I respond by saying it's 'really unusual. Is yours Irish?' another student chimes in with 'don't try and spell it that's all I'm saying!' and Clodagh simply says, 'yeah, Irish'. This is an exchange I recognise (having a Welsh name no one can spell) and feel guilty for instigating. The group are friends and Clodagh is not visibly upset but nonetheless she is marked out as different by me and then by her friend. Her Irish identity is touched upon later in the transcript too when we discuss the choice of music:

Callum:	The music – that was insane just something so there just so right.
Several:	[over the top of Callum]: Yeah, the music was great.
Several:	The singing was very good/beautiful.
John:	Harmonies.
Clodagh:	Because it was the kind of music as well like the um Gaelic, I would say Gaelic but–
John:	The harmonies sound like instruments,
Callum:	Gaelic, yeah.
Me:	Gaelic's Scotland, you see, and Irish is Gaelic.
Clodagh:	Yeah, so I, I found that really interesting 'cause when we watched the film of it it is set in Scotland and it sort of brought, it made me feel–
Callum:	See I didn't see the relevance of that until after, until it was explained and I thought: Yeah, it all makes sense.

Clodagh: It was really, really clever 'cause you like see something then you research into it and it brings a whole different meaning to what you saw. I'm gonna use that in my uni interview [all girls laugh].

Callum: I just thought it worked so well.

The conversation refers to the music in the production broadly at first, then becomes more clearly to do with the singing in the production. Clodagh then particularly mentions the fact that Gaelic is used in the production. She pronounces the name of the language as though it is Irish Gaelic and I then differentiate between the Scottish and Irish pronunciations of the word in English. Clodagh never tells us what the Scottish setting made her think when she first watched it, but she is linking the setting of the play to the music and showing that she understood why Gaelic might have been used in the production. She also tells us that knowing that Gaelic had been chosen gave 'a whole different meaning to what you saw'. Whilst it is a shame that Callum interrupts her at this point, we do see a flicker of personal connection to the play that comes from her Irish heritage, provoked by the subtle references to Scotland included in Audibert's choice of music.

All the students in the group seem to agree that the music was powerful and 'worked so well' within the play. What should be noted is that this use of Gaelic in productions of *Macbeth* is rare. Sìm (2014) suggests that any translation of *Macbeth* into Gaelic, or indeed productions that utilise Gaelic, 'become a space in which to reflect on both the historical and ongoing prejudice about the language and its culture' (31). Clodagh's 'I would say Gaelic', is a way in which she positions herself as part of a minority of Irish speakers. Her differentiation between the pronunciation of the two languages does not dismiss Scottish Gaelic as unconnected but suggests that she sees them as different versions of the same thing. Despite living in the north-east of England, she chooses in this moment to emphasise her connection to a minority language and culture and thus to identify with another, closely linked minority language and culture. Innes' work draws attention to the derision by the National English-speaking Scottish press of those wanting to develop Scottish Gaelic as a language in Scotland. Putting Gaelic on the English National Theatre's stage is, therefore, another bold gesture that this production makes.

Using Gaelic within a production of *Macbeth* foregrounds the Scottish setting of the play. Shakespeare's writing does this, arguably, by drawing on stereotypes of the Scottish as barbarous compared to the English. Cinematic productions such as Kurzel's (2015) use landscapes on location throughout their films. This production, however, uses the music to create a sense of place at two moments within the play. The singing occurs during the murders of Banquo and Lady Macduff and her son. Because Banquo was acted by and as a woman, the female vocals, in Scottish, are played over the screams of two women who are murdered as they try to save their children. The melancholy music adds to the pathos of both scenes but also parallels them clearly for the audience. The audience, at Dunsinane, unable to understand the language, call it 'beautiful' and mention the 'harmonies'. Without knowing that the lyrics of the song are in Gaelic, it does not take on relevance to the setting of the story. The use of a language other than English is to some extent appropriated to add to an atmosphere rather than for what the voice or lyrics might actually be saying. That Scotland is alluded to in these two violent moments in such mournful tones echoes the sentiments of Malcom and Macduff's laments in Act 4 scene iii. The music reflects the downfall of Scotland as a kingdom, aligned as it is with the fatal cries of Banquo and Lady Macduff. The juxtaposition of violence with the specifically Gaelic music provides a counter voice to the presentation of the Scottish as inherently violent, rather emphasising the weeping country in the face of one tyrannical king. The poignancy of the music pleases Clodagh who was glad to be associated, as someone who identified as Irish Gaelic, with the music everyone admired.

'Just a Woman Here, Someone Gay There'

I will turn now to the conversations the groups had about gender and sexuality. Once again, we see that the young audiences are highly engaged with the casting. Their discussions are wide ranging and suggest that the play provoked serious consideration of the theme of gender in *Macbeth* but also of wider societal attitudes towards the topic.

All three excerpts from the interviews I will refer to here include positive comments about the fact that women played men in the production: 'I like the way Banquo and Macduff were played by women' (Aki). 'I like how it had same sex couples' (Brida). 'It's nice seeing representation and stuff' (Amelia). However, this positivity about the general principle is met with varying degrees of scepticism in all three conversations. This questioning of how and why the gender swaps were done appears to come from tension between the perceived context of Shakespeare's writing and the contemporary moment. Threaded through all three conversations are complex ideas about whether and how the switching of gender affected their experience of watching the play. All the conversations acknowledge that the gender swaps are, to some extent, meant to represent modernity and yet there are questions from the groups about what that modernising choice does to the play and to the audience.

When exploring performances of Shakespeare where there is cross-gendered casting, there is, as James C. Bulman (2008) notes in the introduction to *Shakespeare Re-dressed*, a temptation to 'historicize a practice which, for today's audiences, would have a radically different significance from what it had four hundred years ago' (56). When looking at the conversations my participants had, cross-gendered casting is situated in a liminal area somewhere between historical authenticity and an attempt to bring the play up to date.

The modernity of gender switching is often used to contribute to the universality of Shakespeare's plays, particularly when trying to appeal to young audiences. The comedies often explore this casting concept due to Shakespeare's inclusion of gender switching and dress up. The 2017 summer season at Shakespeare's Globe presented *Twelfth Night* as a play that speaks to gender non-conforming youth. The Globe's promotional materials presented Shakespeare's comedies as speaking from 1600s gender non-conformity to the one in ten youths in 2018 who identify the same way. Kemp argues that although there is cross-dressing and queering of roles within plays such as *Twelfth Night* and *As You Like It*, the plays do not present a version of the lived experience that is recognisable to today's queer, trans and non-binary people (Kemp, 2019: 120). This critique does not suggest that Shakespeare failed to represent this experience properly, but that a modern theatre seeking to make a link between Shakespeare's characters that cross-dress or transvestitism and the modern trans experience is naïve at best and at worst a marketisation of queer experience that misunderstands the true trauma and struggle of those experiences. Better perhaps, Kemp says, to look to the plays where themes like sexual assault, homelessness and dysphoria are raised than ones where there is cross-dressing. Kemp's closing argument is that 'it seems important to create scholarship that is rooted in experience, not abstraction' (125).

When the audience members discuss the gender switching in *Macbeth*, there is, in some of the conversations, a recognition of the fact that not only have the genders changed but in the case of Macduff, this ostensibly means the introduction of a lesbian couple to the play's narrative. When I asked about this choice in the Q&A sessions held after most of the performances, the students' answers varied. In one school, the answer was simply 'why not?' whereas in another the answer was that the futuristic, post-apocalyptic transposition allows for the bending of rules on who can be what – so women can be warriors. The students are unhappy with the generic answer to the question about the transposition. The idea that to have a lesbian couple in the play must be something of the near and dystopian future does not sit well with them: 'why can't it just be now?' seems a fair question.

In the following excerpts, I will look at how groups from Cawdor and Dunsinane responded to the casting. We will see that these young people interrogate the casting choices through a range of lenses, drawing on their own experiences of the world and of Shakespeare. Unifying threads run through the three conversations about expectations, authenticity, and representation. As with the conversations about colour-blind casting, the way in which these intertwine creates far more nuanced responses to this aspect of casting than might be expected from the young audiences. Whilst the casting choices are overwhelmingly welcomed, there are questions to be answered.

Victory for Women

Aki: I liked the way that Banquo and Macduff were played
                        by women. It shows like the different aspects of er,
                        equality. It doesn't always have to be men to play male
                        characters. And two of the witches were male as well,
                        and in the play they're both female.

Me:	And what sort of point did you think they were trying to make? Anyone can answer that.
Anselm:	That the play *Macbeth* can be done by anyone.
Vince:	I don't think it can.
Me:	You don't think it can?
Vince:	Nah.
Me:	So you disagree with Aki. That's fine; that's absolutely fine. What made you disagree with it?
Vince:	It's cuz if someone's called Lord Macbeth and one's called Lady So and So the man should be played by a man in my opinion. Because if a man played a woman it would be seen as [several students are laughing/trying to interrupt him and I interject and say 'let Vince speak'] it's like if a man plays a woman it's always seen as wrong but if a woman plays a man it's always seen as a victory for women.
Several students:	That's true; I see that [etc.].
Anselm:	Didn't during Shakespeare's time everyone was played by men so all the female parts were played by men?
Vince:	Yeah, and that's looked upon as wrong, but when it's done in our time, if it was all women played it be like oo la la victory for women, they can do, they–
Jemma:	It's because of the past.
Vince:	Yeah, but the past's the past, it shouldn't dictate what we see as now. If a man plays a woman it's seen as oh the men get all the good parts but if a woman plays a man it's a victory for women.
Jemma:	That's because they weren't allowed before, and that's why it's seen as victory.
Aki:	That's true in Shakespeare times all the female parts were played by males instead of females; there was no female actors and stuff.
Adam:	They all cut their things off. Some men cut their things off so they could–[Laughter]

| JJ: | Basically what he means, yeah, they used to cut their tings off yeah [laughter] so their voice didn't break, to hit the high notes. |
| Me: | So, not their whole 'ting' but their testicles. |

The group from Cawdor are dominated by the voice of one boy, Vince. Vince's opinion that 'if someone's called Lord Macbeth and one's called Lady So and So, the man should be played by a man in my opinion' goes against Aki's opening comment on the topic, 'I liked the way Banquo and Macbeth were played by women.' The group dynamics appear to shape what happens next, with a tentative negotiation of Vince's forthright conviction following. At first, his point of view is met with laughter and interruptions. As the interviewer, I have to ask them to let him carry on speaking. As he continues, the students modify their responses, nodding along with him and agreeing. 'That's true; I see that.'

Anselm's interjection is not a direct response to Vince, but it is a probing statement that can be read as questioning Vince's anger at the women playing men; however, his language does not directly challenge Vince. His response to the stage history (of men playing women's parts) seems to add to Vince's frustration: 'yeah and that's looked upon as wrong, but when it's done in our time, if it was all women played, it'd be like oo la la victory for women, they can do, they'. This 'victory for women' phrase is used three times. It signifies, I think, that Vince sees the casting of women in men's roles as a direct challenge to men. The 'oo la la' in this moment is said in a high-pitched tone that I think is meant to be feminine.

Where Anselm chose to be assertive, but not directly contradict Vince, the next response comes from Jemma, who does directly challenge him, but very quietly. 'It's because of the past', she almost whispers as though unsure of herself or, perhaps, of Vince's reaction or indeed, sure of her point, but not feeling the need to call it out. Her point that 'they weren't allowed before' follows on from Anselm's but offers a little more. The idea that women were not allowed, rather than just that men did play female parts, is a subtly different angle on the same point. Indeed, Vince does agree with her: he says, 'yeah', but continues to argue that the past 'shouldn't dictate what we see as now'. That men might have to give up 'the good parts' for, as Aki put it, 'different aspects of equality' to be seen is a real problem for Vince.

Though ostensibly talking about who should play who in *Macbeth*, what Vince appears to be doing in the conversation is voicing his feelings about feminism in society. Jemma's simple explanation of the narrative of oppression that justifies a celebration of females taking over male roles is an argument that is played out in society at large. John Yandell (2013) suggests that the reading of a text can allow students to talk about issues that are important to them or possibly even painful to them through literature (75–90). In this conversation, a cursory knowledge of theatre history and this performance of *Macbeth* has allowed all the participants to talk about gender through the issues of the past, the staging conditions in the present and the fictional characters of Shakespeare's text.

At this point in the discussion, several other students become involved and the shaky understanding they have of historical performance leads the conversation down a slightly giggly route that alleviates some of the tension created between Jemma and Vince. The discomfort felt throughout this conversation and the tonal shifts are fascinating. Despite the silliness, this part of the conversation does suggest a different kind of issue with cross-gendered casting for Adam and JJ. Their discomfort, even in jest, is not with female actors playing men but at the idea of men playing women. Their anxiety about this aspect of performance history manifests in an ill-informed discussion of castration. The whole conversation centres around the way these young men feel about the loss of something historically masculine. Despite not knowing much about the actual performance of boy actors or castrato singers, enough of this cultural history and modern discussions of gender equality have permeated their London classroom that they bring it with them to discuss the performance of *Macbeth*.

There Were Just Questions

The following exchange between Clodagh and Iris continues the theme of relevancy and modernity in relation to cross-gendered casting. However, it goes deeper than questions of representation and attempts to consider the ways in which casting might alter the meaning of the play. Indeed, it brings to the fore the question of whether there is an essential meaning to the play that can be obscured by casting. When she says, 'are you just doing it because it's trendy at the moment', she is somewhat withering, but her comment becomes profound in its desire to find the 'moral' and 'knowledge of Shakespeare'.

Clodagh:	I really liked it, yeah, I just couldn't, like, why did, do you know, I just wasn't sure about, like, why they, it's like, whenever things are transposed into like dystopia setting, it always feels like why what does that bring to it, and gen – masculinity in Macbeth has always been something I thought that's why Lady Macbeth is so startling because she's a woman whereas they changed that and Macduff was a woman. Banquo's a woman; throughout I was thinking why have they done that and what does it bring to the story and the moral of it?
Me:	Did you, did you think it took away from the moral of it?
Clodagh:	No no 'cause I think in Shakespeare it's ambiguous, it means what you want it to mean in a way but um I was just wondering throughout, and why, why was the witches over a radioactive waste pot, like, I was just thinking like.
Me:	Just why?
Clodagh:	Yeah! but I did like it, it's just there were just questions.
Iris:	It's like whenever things are transposed it's like are you doing that because it's trendy at the moment or is it because it's relevant to the knowledge of Shakespeare.

Clodagh's primary concern is with the repositioning of Lady Macbeth in a world where Banquo and Macduff are also women. Her description of Lady Macbeth as 'so startling because she's a woman', is clearly a personal reading of the character developed through studying the play. I am interested in what she means by 'the moral' of the play and how switching the gender of male characters might change what she perceives the moral to be. Her answer that the meaning is 'ambiguous' might suggest she is using moral interchangeably with meaning. Perhaps, then, we might infer that there is a message being conveyed through either Lady Macbeth's relative isolation as a woman or her inclusion amongst a range of women in the play. Clodagh can see that there might be room for this version of the play ('it means what you want it to mean'), but that such a change cannot be taken lightly.

As Clodagh's reservations highlight, the question of the performance of the female Macduff and Banquo, is not as simple as whether it makes sense to have women as warriors. It is not a production that transforms the roles into performatively feminine ones. We are also reminded here of Kemp's discussion of how and why queer relationships are presented on stage in Shakespeare. This is not a production that portrays a clearly queer relationship between Macduff and Lady Macduff. Both women play hardy warriors who, despite the female pronouns used, are presented as having the same lifeworlds as Shakespeare's Banquo and Macduff and carry themselves in a way that is more performatively militaristic and arguably masculine. Banquo, with long hair and a curvaceous figure, authentically inhabits a world where her gender has not confined her success as a warrior despite her at some point in the past also having become a mother to Fleance. The fact that Macduff and Lady Macduff are never seen on stage together also creates a sense that the supposedly lesbian presence within the play is not based on and does not present, or is not drawn from, an 'experience' of being lesbian. Thus, although there are portrayals of warrior-mothers and a loving lesbian relationship, these are, perhaps, rooted in abstraction and not experience and therefore the transformation of these characters into women feels somewhat incomplete. As Clodagh asks, 'why have they done that?'

It is arguable that the lack of explanation for Banquo's motherhood and the absence of any sexual or loving contact between Macduff and her Lady was an attempt to close the 'gap' between the female bodies and their male characters (Klett, 2009: 31–56). Yet the use of the female pronouns and ambiguous physical presentation makes this closure incomplete. We might return to Kemp's point (and one made in the transcripts) that in fact it is through Lady Macbeth that Shakespeare explores the experience of being 'startling', gender non-conforming or even suffering dysphoria within a hyper-masculine world. By casting Banquo and Macduff as women, Lady Macbeth's predicament is undermined as she claims she would do all sorts of things if she were a man when, in the world into which the play has been transposed, women do all those things anyway. Whilst it may be 'a nice thing to see', there are issues with gender switching the characters in the play as opposed to using gender 'blind' casting but keeping the pronouns.

Both Clodagh and Iris seem sceptical of changes that appear to pander to a modern audience. Clodagh emphasises her point that the production raised questions by asking 'why, why was the witches over a radioactive waste pot?' and this seems to chime with the rather arch comment about trendiness from Iris. Both recognise the potential of changes to bring about insight into the play or 'the knowledge of Shakespeare', but in meddling with the casting of the production, masculinity, a key theme in Clodagh's eyes, needs to be properly considered. Her repetition of 'why' highlights what is important to her as an audience member watching a production that has been designed to be unconventional.

As the students from Dunsinane continue to discuss the production, what does become apparent is that they appreciated the representation of 'LGBT' and 'same sex couples', even if it was not done with as much thought as Clodagh would have liked in relation to *Macbeth* as a story. The way they describe society, as I mentioned earlier in this section, appears somewhat naïve for the students in the discussion:

Amy: In 2017 LGBT community all this like 'there's no minorities any more, everyone is equal' [a few voices agree with her as she speaks] it's crazy to think that the same sex couples in *Macbeth* would be so, d'you know what I mean, alien to us, and yet I mean, there's people here that are homosexual, and that's not a thing, nobody's bothered, and to see it in that and be acted with, and everyone runs with it it's, I think it's interesting. I know, I suppose you could, like, include that in transposing it but it was just it was cool, it was a cool thing to look at.'

Her matter-of-fact tone and earnest belief that being homosexual is 'not a thing' and that 'nobody's bothered' is a reflection driven by the earlier conversation about how surprising it is to see same sex couples on stage. Whether those same sex couples do something to the play itself is not her point here; it is simply that the idea of homosexuality 'being acted with' is a positive thing. When she says, 'I suppose you could, like, include that in transposing,' she tentatively suggests that it need not be considered a part of the play-world and might be seen more as a nod to the real world where we can 'act *with*' and 'run *with*' homosexuality rather than excluding same sex couples from the stage.

Conclusions

What the National Theatre achieved through casting against tradition was important, even if flawed in some regards. As outlined in Section 1 of this Element, the way in which Shakespeare has been framed for school audiences over time has not required students to experience or give much thought to Shakespeare in performance. How watching a production makes an audience feel about themselves and reflect on the world around them is something that has become increasingly present in examiners reports (AQA, 2023). However, with a heavy focus on a deficit model of young people's cultural capital still the prevalent discourse from the DfE (as explored in Section 1 of this Element), it is far from a given that context of reception or reader and audience response are considered in the planning of English literature lessons. When we listen to their conversations after watching the play, we see that they have real, serious thoughts about Shakespeare, performance and the society in which they live.

As well as considering some of their perspectives on this particular production, we see how important what we show our students actually is and how a discussion of a text in performance has the potential to provoke connections between texts and students' worlds that go far beyond any kind of cynical relevancy. What we show them matters to them and can influence how they interact with the texts we put in front of them. It can be difficult, for us as teachers, to introduce students to Shakespeare's plays in ways that speak to them, particularly through casting. The RSC cast Reuben Joseph as Macbeth in 2023 and Shakespeare's Globe had a diverse cast including the main parts for *Romeo and Juliet* in 2021. These two plays loom large in classrooms and those two playhouses do too with enormous amounts of outreach work conducted across the country. But access to live theatre is not financially or geographically possible for many schools. Furthermore, the ways in which they interact with Shakespeare in performance are far from straightforward whether at the theatre or in the classroom. Teachers like Charlotte Dixey, as we shall see, show how performance can be included as an object of and way into analytical thought, but it is nonetheless true that despite these great efforts we are limited in what we can show and therefore the choices we make about which productions, where and when we show them, is crucial.

The position of Shakespeare as a national icon and symbol of British culture is reinforced by his place as the only named writer on the UK National Curriculum and a compulsory element of all GCSE Literature qualifications (Coles, 2013; DES, 1989; DfE, 2014; Yandell, 2016; Yandell, 2017). Seeing themselves represented in *Macbeth* appears to allow students like Jay, Bella, Clodagh and Iris to connect to Shakespeare in ways that surprised them (*Teaching Shakespeare 22*, 2022; *Shakespeare Survey 74*, 2021). Knowing that parts of their identity that had, in their varied levels of experience, excluded them from identifying with Shakespeare's work, could, in fact, be easily included, is important. To feel seen whilst watching something with such cultural weight and so closely attached to their own future success is evidently positive for these groups of students.

3 For Some Must Watch, While Some Must Sleep: Awakening Students' Critical Voices Using Gregory Doran's *Hamlet* (2009)

This section focuses on the use of Gregory Doran's film version of *Hamlet* and how I used it to teach A-Level students the value of adaptation and interpretation. Whilst Section 2 examined post-show discussions about directorial choices, this section will involve more anecdotal reflections following the teaching of an SoW delivered to seventeen- and eighteen-year-olds. This SoW was designed to show students how watching performances could facilitate their reading of scholarship and critical thought. The aim was that viewing performance could enable students to become metacognitive about their own learning and awaken their own critical voices. It is my hope that other practitioners may become similarly reflective about teaching 'critical interpretations' as part of the A-Level syllabus and beyond. What unites both this section and Section 2, however, is the underlying desire for students to become active spectators of Shakespeare's work.

My first encounter of teaching A-Level students to think critically took place in my first year of teaching at a school in West London. A-level, or Advanced level, is the examination students take in their final year at high school. English literature is not a compulsory subject – none of them are – but it is frequently taken as an additional arts A-Level by students who are more interested in other subjects as well as by those with a special aptitude for English. Typically, students study for three A-levels and in exceptional circumstances four. At my particular school, A-Level classes were organised by ability – the most able students, with the highest current grades and internal target grades, were placed in Set 1, and those who had lower targets or current grades were placed in subsequent sets.[4] Arriving at the school as a newly qualified teacher, I had inherited a Set 3 Year 13 class (where the students are seventeen and eighteen years old) which had the lowest target grades of the Year 13 English Literature cohort. The Year 13 class of fifteen students was genuinely interested in English and generally enjoyed discussion and opinion-based tasks. It was clear that they had the germs of critical voices within them but that this needed refinement. Whilst the class was incredibly endearing, they struggled with independent study and the organisation of their ideas – this was compounded by attendance issues within the class. Their end of Year 13 target grades ranged from Ds to a majority of Cs and Bs, with two or three students expected to achieve As, the top grade bar one, which is A*.

The A-Level curriculum had just undergone a national change and there was a general feeling that although our *Hamlet* Year 13 SoW had been implemented and successfully enabled exploration of the play, there were still areas to work on. Among these, most significantly, addressing the 'different interpretations' assessment objective became a priority. This assessment objective (AO5) – there are five in total – is a key element of the Pearson Edexcel Drama component (Pearson being the examining body for the A-Level course we had chosen).[5] When designing our A-Level curriculum, we wanted to blend a fundamental

---

[4] Internal target grades are indicators of what students could achieve at the end of the academic year. They are intended to provide students with a glimpse of what their potential could be and are often aspirational.

[5] AO5 reads: 'Explore literary texts informed by different interpretations'. See the Pearson Edexcel A-Level English Literature Specification (https://qualifications

understanding of the text itself with resources which would ready students for the requirements of the exam they would sit at the end of Year 13. Students were as yet unfamiliar with the 'different interpretations' part of the Pearson syllabus because the Poetry and Prose components, taught in Year 12, were not explicitly assessed for this assessment objective but for AO4, for example, where they were assessed on their ability to 'Explore connections across literary texts'. As each A-Level class had two teachers, each teacher would cover roughly half of the course content. Therefore, whilst Year 13 students were being taught *Hamlet* (the set Shakespeare text for the Drama component) by Teacher A, they would also be studying their Coursework unit with Teacher B at the same time.[6] As both the Drama and Coursework components are assessed for AO5 ('different interpretations') students would be taught this new skill simultaneously by both teachers in the first weeks of Year 13.

In their A-Level Drama paper (Pearson Edexcel GCE English Literature specification) students are expected to answer one question from a choice of two questions concerning their set Shakespeare text. Their answer is then examined for argument in response to the question and text, references to key moments in the play, analysis of the key ideas, understanding of the contextual factors of the time, and engagement with secondary criticism. The latter item is framed as 'critical material' and Edexcel provides schools with suggested readings which complement the text choices supplied by the exam board (Pearson Edexcel AS and A Level English Literature Shakespeare Critical Anthology). As well as a general section on the genre of tragedy, featuring voices such as David Scott Kastan and A. C. Bradley, the anthology comprises three critical articles for each set Shakespeare text that schools could have chosen. For *Hamlet*, students are given essays by John Kerrigan, Janet Adelman and William Hazlitt. Throughout this section, any reference to 'critical perspectives' or 'critical interpretations' echoes the language of

.pearson.com/content/dam/pdf/A%20Level/English%20Literature/2015/
Specification%20and%20sample%20assessments/gce2015-a-level-eng-lit-spec.pdf).

[6] The Drama component of the qualification states that it is compulsory to study one Shakespeare play as well as another play from a range of playwrights including Oscar Wilde, Tennessee Williams and Christopher Marlowe.

the mark scheme supplied by the exam board and I will use the terms 'critical perspectives' and 'critical interpretations' with this in mind rather than any other.

First Steps

Furnished with the exam board's Critical Anthology, I set about teaching the academic articles found therein, mostly through emphasising the need to memorise key quotations from these articles in isolation, having hurriedly read through the entire article with the students in class with little exploration of each article's key ideas and arguments because of the constraints of time. As a result, I naïvely trusted that the class would be able to imitate this process independently at home by working through the remaining articles in the anthology. At this point in the autumn term, we had been studying *Hamlet* for a few weeks already and teaching the first article had to coincide with setting up their first internally assessed essay which would be completed at home.[7] This particular essay would be internally and formatively assessed for every assessment objective in the unit, something that students would be doing for the first time.

In hindsight, this was a tall demand; this assessed essay was initially designed to give us formative feedback on the students and how well they had understood this new assessment object. For my class in particular, with only a few weeks of teaching behind them, this was incredibly challenging. Not only were they being tasked with reading and understanding quite a challenging and complex play, one of Shakespeare's most philosophical dramas, they were also expected to marry their understanding of a primary text to secondary sources in a limited time frame. Consequently, with the benefit of more practical A-Level teaching experience behind me, I soon realised how daunting a prospect this must have been for students: the mammoth task of first understanding the premise of what literary theory was, and why it was important; comprehending the key concepts of a secondary critic after working their way through academic syntax and vocabulary; navigating how to apply theory to a challenging play; applying established critical judgements alongside their own argument (in

---

[7] As per the school's internal assessment calendar.

a sophisticated way) to 'illuminate [their] own critical position' (Edexcel mark scheme for the A-Level Drama paper). I did not quite appreciate the gravity of these challenges before I started teaching them – as such, refining the way I taught critical theory and interpretation became a key focus for me for the duration of that year and the years to come. For a class like the one I had in my Newly Qualified Teacher (NQT) year, secondary sources were too abstract on paper and too challenging to comprehend in isolation. They were also too far removed from the students' own understanding of the play and the language too difficult to navigate. I was adamant that there must be a way I could differentiate such difficult concepts in a more visual and engaging way so as not to alienate my students from their studies and the world of literature at large – I had already introduced the idea of interpretation in a vague way by showing them clips of performances to enhance their understanding of the text, but I felt that this approach was rather limited and that I hadn't fully refined what I could get out of them.

Making Changes

The following year I taught the same scheme of work, with some minor alterations, to a very different, higher-ability Year 13 class. This class of eighteen students had end of Year 13 targets of A*s, As and Bs. They were far more independent learners than the class of the previous year, and very aspirational. In the same year, I was assigned the departmental development task of editing the existing *Hamlet* SoW, with a view to incorporating critical ideas in lessons earlier in the SoW, developing opportunities for extended writing in lesson time, unpicking more model answers and finding more critics to be used in tandem with the ones supplied by the exam board. This was designed to address student outcomes, as our department analysis of our previous year's A-Level results showed that our students struggled to pick up marks for AO5 ('different interpretations') across the board.

Consequently, having taught this unit to both a lower-ability and higher-ability class, I considered how to make the teaching of this assessment objective more engaging and pondered how the study of critical thought could aid students to become critical thinkers themselves. My main priority was that no student should be alienated by the study of critical language or concepts. An integral part of this was to consider how the exam board's Critical Anthology could be used as a springboard for understanding interpretations of Shakespeare elsewhere – on the stage or on film, for example. I pondered how to make the work of these established literary scholars less abstract, both to support lower-ability students but also to challenge the higher-ability ones. I began to consider what the word 'interpretation' meant, and whether we had to be confined to written articles. From my experience of teaching secondary school Shakespeare up until that point, I knew students engage positively when considering directorial choices, and this led me to wonder whether I could utilise this approach alongside an examination of academic reading; I wondered how far performance could enhance the understanding of both primary and secondary texts. At the same time, I felt it was important to marry the specifications of the exam board's mark scheme to diverse readings of the text, enabling students to articulate their own views of such a canonical play. In short, it was key to 'read' performances first which would enable students to return to the text with a critical lens. After all, 'there can never be a performance of Shakespeare that is not at the same time an *interpretation* of Shakespeare' (Reynolds, 1991: 199).

I soon felt strongly that performance-based activities could help to develop the critical voices of these Year 13 students because it would break down any preconceived barriers between the academic world and each student's reality. I wanted to foster an appreciation of interpretation in them. As well as this, I knew these types of activities would have a more lasting effect on students and they were more likely to remember performances they had seen and unpicked than obscure texts they had hurriedly read.

In conversation with my current Year 13 class (academic year 2021–2), I asked if they could remember a performance that best encapsulated what an interpretation was. Orlando, a student who struggles with processing ideas and is dyslexic, charted a few examples: 'The *Hamlet* one with the audience ... the tall audience ... and Hamlet was being aggressive and loud, versus the David Tennant one in a small room with small people ... it made him look more hysteric[al] and crazy'. This student was referring to the stately setting of Kenneth Branagh's *Hamlet* (1996) juxtaposed with the relative intimacy of Gregory Doran's adaptation (2009). Orlando had clearly elicited some key ideas about how the directors differed in their staging of the text – the impact of stage levels, tonal details, contrast and characterisation, to name a few. Orlando's response illuminates the barrier I wanted to break down; by creating visual aids and considering directors as critics, I estimated that students would better comprehend why and how critics were writing, and how they had formed their interpretation of the play. It was essential to examine the purpose of critical thought before we launched into an analysis of different critical voices in essay writing. For a student like Orlando, this would make challenging essay writing skills more accessible. For many students, as the practised teacher well knows, without any context, it is difficult to think, discuss or write with purpose or efficacy. As well as building in these ideas earlier in the SoW, with more time devoted to unpicking critical ideas, we hoped student confidence about these higher-level skills would grow and begin to flourish.

The 'Mechanics of the Play'

English teachers might have some hesitancy about using performance to explore a text. I discussed the merits and hurdles of using performance in English lessons with an experienced colleague, Jack, who has been both a head of English and a head of film studies in his career. In response to a question about the benefits of teaching through Shakespeare performance, he said:

> You can see the mechanics of the play ... the difficulty is, I suppose, it's ideal to see it on the stage performed in the theatre as it works, whereas in film there are so many cheats that you can use, or too much modernisation or weirdness to it. .... But the main advantage is ... seeing a lot of interactions between the characters that aren't always in the words themselves – the way they react to each other because of what they're saying ... and I think that emotional ... all the negative space where there [are] no words at all ... the reaction ... helps students to understand one particular interpretation of what's happening between characters.

The 'negative space' he refers to was what I hoped my students would benefit from seeing, and, indeed, I knew they had missed this in our hurried first readings of the play. This absence was felt in turn by students. When I asked my current Year 13 students how they responded to the use of performance in their learning, one student, Juliet, who struggles to articulate her initial ideas about a text, echoed my colleague's feelings about the power of a text in action: 'It helps your understanding . . . what you're watching. For example, tone of voice may help you understand the key message more than just reading it.' I felt it was crucial for students to have more room for exploration so they could examine the 'mechanics' of the play and its resonances, simultaneously sculpting their own views of how the play operates in practice, and identifying how others, in an academic world, perceived similar things. For them, we could labour and annotate the play on paper to our heart's content, but their fundamental knowledge of the primary text would come to fruition only once we had seen it in action, because, as my colleague Mark stated, 'the play almost doesn't exist until it is performed'.

I had chosen Gregory Doran's 2009 RSC rendition of *Hamlet* as my main teaching tool. This adaptation was re-staged for television, broadcast on BBC2, having previously been performed in Stratford-upon-Avon and London in 2008. The original stage version was a sell-out success and David Tennant, in the starring role, received favourable reviews. As such, I hoped the recognisable faces in the production would elicit student 'buy in', but I also wanted an adaptation that was invariably 'modern' to pique the students' interest. The BBC2 production also examines the nature of surveillance in an original way which the confines of the stage version could not. There are moments when we view the castle of Elsinore through CCTV footage and when Hamlet breaks the fourth wall by staring intently into his own film camera. The production found thought-provoking ways to convey ideas about secrecy, trust and surveillance with clarity. Additionally, Hamlet films other characters, notably during the Mousetrap scene, explicitly reinforcing the duplicity between outward appearance and inward emotion. The editing of camera shots and angles also bears huge significance for building student understanding because Doran so perfectly demonstrates how spying, voyeurism and control infuse the play. I felt that it was an appropriate adaptation that didn't do what my colleague Jack warned about: I didn't feel as if the editing took anything away from the text's core meaning, and the modernisation certainly didn't feel like inorganic 'cheats' that bore no resemblance to our study of the play. This take on surveillance, which I will explore in more depth later on in this section, set Doran's work apart from any other adaptation of *Hamlet* I had seen. By focusing on Doran's rendition of *Hamlet*, we hoped, students could identify an alternative interpretation in action, enriching not only their own reading of the play, but breaking down, camera shot by camera shot, how others might read the play too.

Reflections

There are a few things to highlight before I chart some examples of how we initially taught this unit. The examples and reflections listed in what follows are by no means exhaustive and that there are surely more ways to teach these skills. Some of these activities were also crafted by several members of staff as our department works collaboratively on schemes of work; therefore, I do not take full credit for the content of the lessons themselves. These considerations, however, are my own reflections on how these lessons worked with a group of Year 13 students that I taught in 2019, and how they could be adapted further. I also refer throughout the section to comments made by two colleagues, both teachers of English with more than ten years of experience. These comments emerged from individual interviews, where I structured some questions around the topic of secondary criticism but also left room for a more organic discussion about their own pedagogy and opinions on teaching Shakespeare through performance. In addition, I briefly interviewed my current Year 13 class in a group scenario with more structured questions to focus their responses purely on how they were taught secondary sources through performance. This student voice proved helpful when assessing how successful the lessons had been and it allowed me to evaluate how best to improve further in the future. All names, both staff and students, have been anonymised.

In summary, our aims were to use Doran's film to explore key themes across the play, encourage students to identify alternative readings of key moments, deconstruct the concept of interpretation, and teach historical and social contexts. In all these scenarios, the adaptation was paired with one or more critical statements to fluently embed these ideas throughout the SoW and achieve our aim of helping students engage with academic writing. Our hope was that they would become more familiar with critical ideas through frequent exposure to secondary sources. The lesson outlines detailed below are taken from the main SoW, but replicated out of the intended sequence for the purpose of this account. Each lesson is designed to last from fifty to sixty minutes.

As my teaching of the scheme was under way, a few things soon became clear about what would be useful to make explicit to students in advance of the unit. First, I encountered questions about creative license and whether staging choices were 'allowed' because they veered so much from the original staging conditions. Therefore, it would be useful to remind students at the start of the unit that there is no absolute when it comes to staging. In fact, allowing sufficient time to discuss directorial choices could be incredibly revealing for students. In essence, it is the students' role (as critics of the text themselves) to decide how convincing each interpretation is. This would make for good material for an introductory lesson, time permitting. Another concept that would be effective to pre-teach overtly is the idea of looking at a text through specific lenses. This analogy is particularly useful when examining a text from the perspective of a school of thought, such as reading *Hamlet* through a Feminist lens or a New Historicist lens. This analogy works wonders in clarifying how critical ideas frame a primary text in different ways, and so the lens of the metaphorical camera complements what each critic is trying to argue. Additionally, the use of secondary critics helps to add legitimacy to their own studies and helps students to see how their ideas about a play bear relevance within a wider literary context, something which can become an oversight when looking at a text in the confines of a classroom.

What Is an 'Interpretation'?

One of the lessons we created implicitly addressed what an interpretation is but needed explicit pre-teaching before starting. This lesson was originally designed to come at the end of the SoW (lesson 21 of 25) once students had finished reading and annotating the whole play. It was a lesson based on the theme of family in *Hamlet* and the objective was to teach students key context and enable them to evaluate critical interpretations of family dynamics in the play. However, I would argue that a lesson like this, instead of taking place towards the end of the scheme, would work better in a much earlier lesson when students first encounter Act 1, scenes 2–3, which juxtapose Hamlet's family with Polonius's. By moving this lesson earlier in the SoW, students would be introduced to critical ideas much earlier and this would be far more accessible if linked to a relevant moment in the play.

In the original lesson, the starter task included independent reading about historical context, including the concept of primogeniture and family bonds, which students would then apply to the play by discussing Polonius' relationship with his children and Gertrude's vulnerability as an Elizabethan widow. Next, students would read through a multitude of critical quotations on the topic of family bonds. Some of the quotes covered arguments such as 'Polonius is a bad parent' or John Kerrigan's view that Ophelia is 'an instrument of Polonius' plots'. Having read these, students would then be ready to identify where these ideas were present in different clips from relevant moments across the play These clips came from the film adaptations by Olivier (1948), Branagh (1996), Icke and Huw (2017), Zeffirelli (1990) and Doran (2009). Once students had done that, as a consolidation task, they would apply their ideas about this theme by positioning themselves into a freeze frame where they role-played as one of the families from *Hamlet*. As part of this activity, they would have to consider the positioning of the characters, where they would be looking, how they would be positioned in relation to each other, as well as other relevant staging decisions. The plenary task, intended to review that lesson, required students to draw together all the ideas from the lesson, including the critical quotes they encountered earlier, to write an analytical response to an exam question about family relationships. Our school policy dictates that each A-Level lesson should culminate in students being set a homework or 'prep' task which is expected to take an hour to complete. A 'prep' (or homework) task should either consolidate that lesson's learning or set students up with a research task for the next one. In the original lesson, the 'prep' task was to read an article about Elizabeth I and prepare a paragraph on how her position on the throne challenged typical patriarchal values.

Reflecting on this lesson, it is easy to see that it would be far more effective if placed earlier on in the SoW alongside a close analysis of Act 1, scene 2, where the students would first read and discuss the scene as a class, with some reference to key contextual ideas. It would be beneficial then to introduce the concept of interpretation by asking them to compare the different approaches of just three different directors instead of overwhelming them with too many adaptations so early on. I would aim to convey what my colleague Mark aptly referred to as 'a plurality of performance' without overwhelming them. This would also alleviate some of the time pressures we encountered and avoid cognitive overload. To do this, I would recommend using Branagh's more traditional 1996 film, the 2017 video recording of the Almeida Theatre production by Robert Icke and Rhodri Huw, and Doran's 2009 film. These three versions vary so comprehensively that a comparison of the productions would engender fruitful discussions. Comparing three versions early on in the unit would ensure students, as my colleague Jack states, had already 'seen two or three different productions of the same story line . . . what they've done essentially is re-read two or three times in a different mind space, so, automatically you're getting a stronger level of criticism and evaluation and interpretation . . . rather than the first read through where they've made some notes hastily copied off the whiteboard.

Already, then, as they explore the text for the first time, they automatically revisit key moments to consolidate their learning. When I questioned my current Year 13 students about the impact of performance on their understanding of the primary text, Titania, a student who struggles with dyslexia but is confident with her own ideas, commented that 'it opens your eyes to different interpretations and gives you a wider understanding of how others might view a text'. In short, providing students with material that they might otherwise be unfamiliar with could stop them from producing restricted and forgettable analyses and inspire more nuanced approaches.

Having watched each interpretation of 1.2 performed in three different ways, students would be tasked with the following questions: How does each director decide to present the family's relationship? How do they do this through staging choices? What are the key elements that they focus on? An additional task would be to have students hot-seat as each director, positing their intentions and what they wanted to achieve, essentially positioning students to understand directors-as-critics reading the play and how successful this is.

Instead of the barrage of isolated critical quotations I provided students with originally, I would streamline these down to selections from just one or two critics (ideally two with clearly distinct ideas) so students could secure their understanding of their arguments and subsequently apply them more effectively in writing. At this point in the lesson, the teacher would need to outline explicitly that the critic is commenting on the original text, not the performances just viewed, and signal a return to examining the page itself. I would hope that having discussed different interpretations at length earlier in the lesson, students would feel more confident about what critical theory entails and its purpose. Before embarking on any sort of independent writing task, a discussion task here is vital to aid students in deciding how convincing a critic's ideas are, and to set them up with the tools to justify their own opinions about a secondary source. As this would be a plenary task in a lesson which is early in the SoW, it would be necessary to model the application of the critic's ideas by doing writing together as a class (with the teacher modelling and students contributing) as a class, focusing on the confident engagement with AO5 ('different interpretations') as students would not have come across how to do this before. I would hope that following this initial lesson, with more exposure to critical interpretations, students would write more independently as the unit progressed.

Finally, there would be a wealth of ways to adapt the original prep for this lesson to better consolidate ideas about the notion of interpretation. One idea might be to ask students to come up with their own directorial choices for 1.2 and 1.3, thinking about props, costumes, blocking and intonation. The teacher could model this by using Doran's choices as a model which could then help students envisage their own interpretation as a result. They could do this in all manner of creative ways, including annotating an extract of the scene or completing a visual design; however, the emphasis would need to be on the *why* behind their choices in order to make this a truly valuable activity. Alternatively, if wishing to develop a more nuanced approach, students could be tasked with independently searching for their own secondary sources. These further critical ideas could then be relayed back to the class in the next lesson. For a more structured approach to consolidating an engagement with critical nuances, it could be beneficial to supply students with an article and accompanying guided questions to support their understanding. These questions could use Doran's choices as a basis of understanding, using the clips they watched to assist with the texts they had read. These could include the following:

- What is the critic's key idea or approach? How does it differ from Doran's approach? Paraphrase it in your own words.
- How did Doran present the families in 1.2? What does the critic think of the family relationships in this scene? What are the key differences or similarities?
- Can you think of a moment in the play so far that supports this reading of the text?
- If this critic were a director, how might they decide to stage the key moments they write about?
- Can you think of ways to disagree with this critic's ideas?

Overall, I soon came to the realisation that for students to build their confidence with these skills, their exposure to critical ideas had to be carefully structured and streamlined; it was too much for them to grasp too many skills at once and over-complicating things could risk them feeling alienated about a skill they could not afford to bypass. By focusing, early on, on interpretation via various versions of a scene, and marrying this with how critics operate, students would feel more equipped when approaching the rest of the unit, and they would have a more secure understanding of the roles of primary and secondary sources as a result.

Student As Spectator-Critic

To engage fully with the act of watching Shakespeare, we wanted students to become active spectators themselves. We aimed to highlight their role as critical spectators by positioning them as an audience that observed how the characters in the play watched each other. Surveillance, spying and observation are all central ideas in *Hamlet* and Doran's adaptation was a perfect counterpart to the teaching of these themes – in his film, he conveys the power and influence of watching and seeing the truths behind each character's appearances through his directorial choices. Significantly, the use of props and editing makes this theme visually explicit, which would be appealing to students, seeing the act of watching on the 'stage' where they might have overlooked it on the page. For example, Hamlet, played by David Tennant, films himself with a camera during his pivotal soliloquies and we see integral moments in the play established through the use of CCTV cameras. By focusing on who was being watched and why, this adaptation made the theme of surveillance more apparent, which students engaged meaningfully with because they felt more actively involved in the plot.

In Lesson 5 of the original SoW, students would explore the nature of surveillance and spying in Act 3 of the play. They would have already read this part of the play in advance of this lesson. As pre-reading for this lesson, students would complete tasks which taught them Jeremy Bentham's concept of the Panopticon and key ideas from Michel Foucault's (1975) *Discipline and Punish: The Birth of the Prison*. Having read a short summary of the key ideas from these thinkers, students were asked to consider the following questions and to independently apply these to *Hamlet*. They would then bring these ideas to the lesson:

- Is it possible to say that the Danish court in Hamlet functions like a Panoptican? What evidence is there that there is nowhere to hide in the court?
- Which institutions in our society could be said to be constructed in the model of a Panoptican?
- Which parts of Shakespeare's society may have followed this model?
- According to Foucault, 'Panopticism made possible a political take-off in relation to the traditional, ritual, costly, violent forms of power, which soon fell into disuse and were superseded by a subtle, calculated technology of subjection' (p. 221). To what extent does this apply to the structure of *Hamlet* and the contrast between Old Hamlet and Claudius?

At the start of Lesson 5, then, students would discuss how they would ensure power and discipline if they were a leader of a country. To differentiate further, students could be furnished with the following areas to consider: trust, observation, spying, disguise, and how to effectively monitor these. Having brainstormed these issues, students would then discuss the ideas emerging from their pre-reading prep task and this would enable the teacher to address any misconceptions about Foucault's ideas and check understanding.

To further develop these ideas about power and control, and to enable students to visualise these seemingly abstract concepts, the next activity would be to watch a compilation of key moments from the Doran adaptation which highlight the use of CCTV footage and how surveillance is presented in the play. These moments were taken from across the play and students were asked to consider whether it was an effective interpretation of *Hamlet* by answering guided questions such as how spying was presented and whether students could find any examples of voyeurism in the adaptation.

Next, students would consider their knowledge of Act 3 as a whole, and chart who exactly is watching whom in the play with the intention of understanding the power dynamics and characterisation. To further narrow the focus of how surveillance operates in the play, students would explore in groups the ways that Ophelia is spied on in 1.2, 2.1 and 2.2. This extract analysis was designed to develop students' close reading skills and their understanding of power dynamics in the play and how gender and character play a part too.

As a final task, the lesson culminated in a discussion where students considered Shakespeare's presentation of this theme, with emphasis on linking their ideas to Elizabethan context. As a development of this plenary, students were shown a model paragraph where critical theory had already been applied to ideas about surveillance, demonstrating how to do this in essay form. As their prep task, to be completed for their next lesson, they would do some more pre-reading on the origins of Shakespeare's *Hamlet* by reading an article on Saxo Grammaticus' account of the legend of Amleth.

This lesson was well received by students, despite my hesitancies about how challenging it might be, as they appreciated the connections between a contextual understanding, textual analysis and an appreciation of new readings of the play. The references to Foucault augmented their own understanding of the play, as well as refining the sophistication of their initial ideas. It worked well alongside an examination of Acts 2 and 3 and would be best placed as a two-part lesson to ensure sufficient depth of ideas.

When reflecting on some of the practicalities of the lesson, I noticed that some of the lower-ability students could not quite grasp the core principles of Foucault's ideas and so some time spent on identifying other structures in society that might utilise the Panopticon for power and control was useful. We broke down these concepts with an impromptu and organic discussion about social structures such as prisons, even schools, before we applied this knowledge to the play. Although I felt that the pace of the lesson was slowing at this point, I saw these distinctions as invaluable because students could apply the concept more concretely later on as a result. However, I soon discovered that the students were misapplying Foucault's ideas – I had glossed over introducing who he was, the time in which he was writing and the purpose of examining his work in relation to *Hamlet*. Due to this, students were then wrongly assuming that Foucault was a contemporary of Shakespeare. Explicit pre-teaching about the context in which we were using Foucault to illuminate our own ideas about the play, would help to establish his ideas as another way to interpret the play. This was a difficult dynamic to teach and so it would definitely be helpful to use the analogy of 'Foucauldian glasses' in which we watch the play.

Students at this point had assumed we could only use individual critics who had specifically written their interpretations in response to the play, and so this type of lesson helped them to consider the validity of different schools of thought. Students also felt confined to a small selection of critics, mostly because we were, at this point, primarily working with the few critical articles supplied by the exam board. Comments like 'but how do I use Foucault to talk about this other moment in the play?' made me realise I had to teach them when certain ideas were appropriate and relevant rather than using critics as a box-ticking exercise.

A member of my department, Mark, who was teaching a high-ability class of Year 13s that year, commented that his class has been swept up by reading *Hamlet* through a solely Marxist lens because they had ill-conceived ideas about how to use schools of thought with sophistication. Far from enhancing their knowledge of the text, this was starting to impinge on their understanding because they were not considering other elements at play. Consequently, Mark addressed this narrow view with his class, stressing that they had to become more flexible in their understanding of the text.

In conversation with me about teaching critics, he commented that 'if you teach them a wealth of many [critics], it stops them having a limited understanding of the play'. It became apparent, in this case, that discussions about the plurality of meaning in the play would be essential and that without a clear grasp of this, students would not be successful at holistically examining the play and its impact.

I also evaluated the usefulness of the YouTube clip from Doran's adaptation which introduced the lesson. This particular clip was a compilation of key moments regarding the theme of surveillance, and these moments were taken from across the whole play. It was undoubtedly successful as an overview of Doran's interpretation; students produced a brief summary of Doran's approach and how this was evident in key scenes across the play. This engendered lots of apt ideas about interpretation and the surveillance state of Claudius' court – something students could not fully grasp on their reading of the text but could when they saw it in performance. Therefore, they could situate what an interpretation was in concrete, real terms, a concept that was too abstract to grasp before this work.

Admittedly, whilst this initial compilation clip was a good introduction to Doran's work, it was slightly disjointed and as we had not reached reading Acts 4 and 5 of the play yet, some students lost focus when it reached that part of the play. Therefore, it would be key for the teacher to provide narration for these parts of the clip to ensure students could follow along and be overtly told how Doran's choices are significant at the end of the play. Alternatively, selecting the most impactful moment from Acts 2 or 3 and watching this in full might bear more relevance to the objective of the lesson. For instance, one of the tasks designed in the initial SoW was to consider the idea of voyeurism and how Ophelia is spied on. Therefore, to develop this task further, as students watched 2.2. in full, they could analyse the primary text first and then evaluate the efficacy of Doran's directorial choices as an accompanying task.

Finally, with more of a time allowance and potentially stretching this into a two-part lesson, it would be effective to not only show students concrete models about how to apply this knowledge in their essay writing, but to actively encourage them, in groups if necessary, to summarise their ideas in writing. With more time, the teacher could unpick a critical quotation about surveillance that might complement Doran's adaptation, and students would feel more confident incorporating this material into their writing. The model originally supplied in the lesson covered Hamlet and Claudius's conflict well, so students could use this model to write up their ideas about Ophelia which they covered during the main portion of the lesson. This task would allow for dedicated writing time, as students would have already built the foundations of their understanding and would be afforded time to execute this in practice, effectively preparing them for their exam and solidifying their knowledge simultaneously. With differentiated and guided questions in front of them, as well as the support of their peers and of the model paragraph, students should feel comfortable enough to attempt writing critically and analysing critical ideas themselves.

Whilst it seemed at the time that this lesson was content heavy, the outcomes were encouraging – students, becoming more accustomed to a variety of interpretations (from individual critics, directors, and schools of thought) showed more confidence both about the play and different readings of it, and their ability to encompass these challenging ideas in their own writing.

'It Helps Your Own Character'

All in all, whilst reflecting on the approach we took through these lessons, and weighing up student responses when I interviewed them, it seemed to me that they had fully grasped the essence of what it meant to have an interpretation of a play, and that they appreciated how performance could help them understand that further. In conversation with my current Year 13 class, it was clear that they were thinking in metacognitive ways about the learning process they had been through. In response to my question about how performances have influenced their understanding of the primary text, they responded with the following:

Malvolio: It allows you the opportunity when you watch an interpretation of a novel, or a play, to either agree or disagree with that interpretation and what they want [to achieve], and that strengthens your critical views.

Interviewer: What value do you think becoming critical has for you as a person, or as a student?

Orlando:	Having your personal opinion and voice. It helps your own character.
Adriana:	I agree. And it helps you question everything.
Lavinia:	You don't see things on the surface level and you think deeper about things.
Malvolio:	It helps you pick out your own point of view and argument so you're more critical of yourself too, and others.

What became clear to me was how transferable these skills were and how far the value of these skills had been reinforced. Malvolio's comment about interpreting novels as well as plays resonated with me because they were already widening their scope of understanding to other forms and genres and considering where else these skills could take them. It seemed to me that Doran's approach had awakened their critical voices, which they honed during the unit, and boosted the confidence of these students in visceral ways. In conversation with my colleague, Jack, he aptly identified how important it was to overcome students' 'first burden of "this is confusing, I don't know what's going on" that needs to be bridged'. He went on to assert how essential it was to 'get the broad skeleton of the framework out [first] and then start looking at the flesh later on'.

To continue with this idea of 'looking at the flesh' of the play, Doran's production enabled my students to dress the play up in their own terms as well as considering how this might evolve throughout the play. By examining Doran's interpretation, we used the familiar form of performance in order to access an unfamiliar play, with unfamiliar critics. Not only did this ultimately help their progress towards harnessing challenging skills, readying them for the demands of further education, but it had immense value in awakening their own critical voices, and they were able to appreciate the play in its wider literary context as a result.

4 Conclusion

In this Element we have attempted to show the way in which spectator theory can be used pedagogically to generate meaning when teaching Shakespeare. In so doing, we differentiate this form of teaching from one which is essentialist or limiting in its conception of knowledge and culture, specifically pedagogies which exclude performance and focus heavily on historical context and close textual analysis. The teachers involved, Myfanwy Edwards and Charlotte Dixey, have shown how the plays watched – *Macbeth* and *Hamlet* – have multiple meanings that can be taught as well as created in collaboration with the young people in our classrooms.

Their accounts differ. Edwards is looking at how students watch a National Theatre production of *Macbeth*. She is not teaching *Macbeth* to the young people she interviews, but she is still able to present the students' perceptions of the play, their moments of intertextuality, their understandings from their own experiences and how they as spectators understood aspects of the play. Through drawing on their discussions we see how their identities, combined with the performances watched, contribute to both interpretations of *Macbeth* and contemplations on the wider world.

Dixey is also looking at a specific production but rather than considering her students' views on a live performance, she takes a production of *Hamlet* by director Gregory Doran and demonstrates how the use of this one particular version of *Hamlet* can be used within a sequence of lessons to show her A-level class that there are many interpretations of the play. The goal of the sequence is that they can then understand better the idea that literary critics, like directors, have different takes on any given play. What is important is that both Edwards and Dixey are teachers, and both are considering spectator theory in their pedagogy.

Dixey presents us with a scheme of work that inherently relies on the students' ability to make meaning from watching a production of *Hamlet*. Her account of how she compiles a scheme of work, listening to other teachers and students in her writing of it, altering the position of lessons based on the students' understanding, is evidence of the way a good teacher works to incorporate performance into their teaching of Shakespeare. Dixey's is a careful representation of how one can practically approach the teaching of Shakespeare using spectator theory. It may have been useful to recount that Doran's version, using technology, was borrowed from Michael Almereyda's production in 2000, or that the use of CCTV is now found in stage productions, as in Robert Icke's production of *Hamlet*, where again the surveillance at court was continuous. But that would not have been an authentic representation of her experience, nor would it reflect the resources generally available to classroom teachers, who cannot attend or necessarily access, several productions of the many plays they teach. Though websites like Drama Online make this much easier than perhaps it once was, there is still work to be done in supporting teachers to access and utilise the productions of Shakespeare's work.

None of this would have been possible had they taken a more print-text, 'knowledge-based' approach. The teaching of Shakespeare can make notions of audience, of spectator, seem like abstract questions or ones to do with the context of the seventeenth-century Globe. 'What did the groundlings think of the play?' 'Was the porter scene put in for light entertainment after high tragedy?' Yet even in a school which is print-text focused, as with Charlotte Dixey's experience, it is possible to include some aspects of spectator theory even if it is only to make students 'think deeper about things'. In Edwards' section, what is clear is that the opportunity to see one's self, to talk about and frame Shakespeare through one's own experiences can be powerful and a meaningful starting point for exploring Shakespeare's work.

In writing this Element we have focused on classroom teachers who have extended their practice through research, one by doing a PhD, the other through action research (although it is notable that Dixey also completed an MA in Shakespeare studies before beginning teaching). Both have found ways in which spectator theory and its use in practical classroom circumstances have extended both their pedagogical practice and their understanding of Shakespeare's plays in performance. There are always challenges in teaching English but ultimately we do it so that students can engage with the texts, learn from the experience and create their own meaning from his plays.

References

Aebischer, P. (2019). South Bank Shakespeare goes global: Broadcasting from Shakespeare's Globe and the National Theatre. In P. Aebischer, S. Greenhalgh and L. E. Osbourne (eds.), *Shakespeare and the 'Live' Theatre Broadcast Experience*. London: The Arden Shakespeare. Pp. 113–32.

Aebischer, P. (2020). *Shakespeare, Spectatorship and the Technologies of Performance*. Cambridge: Cambridge University Press.

AQA. (2023). www.aqa.org.uk/exams-administration/exams-administration-updates/2022-2023-question-papers,-mark-schemes-and-reports-on-the-exam-whats-available-when. Accessed 6 November 2023.

Baker-Bell, A. (2020). *Linguistic Justice: Black Language, Literacy, Identity, and Pedagogy*. New York: Routledge.

Bennett, S. (2005 (1997)). *Theatre Audiences: A Theory of Production and Reception*. 2nd ed. London: Taylor & Francis Group.

Bennett, S. (2019). Shakespeare's new marketplace: The places of events cinema. In P. Aebischer, S. Greenhalgh and L. E. Osbourne (eds.), *Shakespeare and the 'Live' Theatre Broadcast Experience*. London: The Arden Shakespeare. Pp. 41–58.

Boakye, J. (2019). *Black, Listed*. London: Dialogue Books.

Brady, M. (2015). From Verona to Ramallah: Living in a state of emergency. *Changing English* 22(4), 365–37.

Bulman, J. C. (2008). *Shakespeare Re-dressed: Cross-Gender Casting in Contemporary Performance*. Vancouver, BC: Fairleigh Dickinson University Press.

Chakravarty, U. (2021). What is the history of actors of color performing in Shakespeare in the UK? In A. Thompson (ed.), *The Cambridge Companion to Shakespeare and Race*. Cambridge: Cambridge University Press. Pp. 190–207.

Coles, J. (2013a). 'Every child's birthright'? Democratic entitlement and the role of canonical literature in the English National Curriculum. *Curriculum Journal* 24(1), 50–66.

Coles, J. (2013b). Constructions of Shakespeare in the secondary school curriculum. PhD. King's College London.

Coles, J. (2020). Wheeling out the big guns: The literary canon in the English classroom. In J. Davison and C. Daly (eds.), *Debates in English Teaching*. London: Routledge.

Core Knowledge. www.coreknowledge.org/about-us/e-d-hirsch-jr. Accessed 24 August 2021.

Department for Education (DfE). (2014). *National Curriculum in England: English*. www.gov.uk/government/publications/national-curriculum-in-england-english-programmes-of-study. Accessed 28 January 2022.

Department of Education and Science (DES). (1975). *A Language for Life* [*Bullock Report*]. London: Her Majesty's Stationery Office.

Department of Education and Science (DES). (1989). *English for Ages 5 to 16*. London: Her Majesty's Stationery Office.

Departmental Committee of the Board of Education (1921). *The Teaching of English in England: Being the Report of the Departmental Committee Appointed by the President of the Board of Education to Inquire into the Position of English in the Educational System of England* [*Newbolt Report*]. London: His Majesty's Stationery Office.

Dewey, J. (1916/2004). *Democracy in Education*. Mineola, NY: Dover.

Dewey, J. (1925/1958). *Experience and Nature*. New York: Dover.

Dewey, J. (1934/ 2005). *Art As Experience*. New York: Perigee.

Dewey, J. (1935/1966). *Experience and Education*. London: Collier Books.

Doecke, B. and Mead, P. (2018). English and the knowledge question. *Pedagogy, Culture & Society* 26(2), 249–64.

Eaglestone, R. (2019). *Literature: Why It Matters*. London: Polity.

Eaglestone, R. (2021). *'Powerful Knowledge', 'Cultural Literacy' and the Study of Literature in Schools. Impact 26: Philosophical Perspectives on Education Policy*. London: Wiley.

Edwards, M. (ed.). (2022). *Teaching Shakespeare 22*. Stratford-Upon-Avon: British Shakespeare Association.

Erne, L. (2013). *Shakespeare As Literary Dramatist*. Cambridge: Cambridge University Press.

Escolme, B. (2005). *Talking to the Audience: Shakespeare, Performance, Self*. London: Taylor & Francis Group.

Flores, N. and Rosa, J. (2015). Undoing appropriateness: Raciolinguistic ideologies and language diversity in education. *Harvard Educational Review* 85(2), 149–71.

Foucault, M. (1975). *Discipline and Punish: The Birth of the Prison*. New York: Vintage Books.

Freshwater, H. (2009). *Theatre and Audience*. London: Palgrave Macmillan.

Gibb, N. (2015). How E. D. Hirsch came to shape UK government policy knowledge and the curriculum. In J. Simons and N. Porter (eds.). *A Collection of Essays to Accompany E. D. Hirsch's Lecture at Policy Exchange*. London: Policy Exchange. Pp. 12–20.

Gove, M. (2010). Speech to the Conservative Party Conference. 5 October.

Grier, M. (2021). Are Shakespeare's plays racially progressive? The answer is in our hands. In A. Thompson (ed.), *The Cambridge Companion to Shakespeare and Race*. Cambridge: Cambridge University Press. Pp. 237–53.

Hadfield, A. (2021). Race in Shakespeare's histories. In A. Thompson (ed.), *The Cambridge Companion to Shakespeare and Race*. Cambridge: Cambridge University Press. Pp. 62–76.

Hall, K. (1996). *Things of Darkness: Economies of Race and Gender in Early Modern England*. Ithaca, NY: Cornell University Press.

Harkin, P. (2005). The reception of reader-response theory. *College Composition and Communication*. 56(3), 410–25.

Hirsch, E. D. (1987). *Cultural Literacy: What Every American Needs to Know*. Boston, MA: Houghton Mifflin.

Innes, S. (2014). Shakespeare's Scottish play in Gaelic. *Scottish Language* 33, 26–50.

The Inspiration Trust (2019). www.inspirationtrust.org. Accessed 10 June 2019.

Iser, W. (1978). *The Act of Reading: A Theory of Aesthetic Response*. Baltimore, MD: Johns Hopkins University Press.

Jones, K. (1989). *Right Turn: The Conservative Revolution in Education*. London: Vintage.

Kemp, S. K. (2019). 'In that dimension grossly clad': Transgender rhetoric, representation, and Shakespeare. *Shakespeare Studies* 47, 113–20.

Klett, E. (2009). The king's many bodies: Fiona Shaw's *Richard II* (1995–96). In E. Klett (ed.), *Cross Gender Shakespeare and English National Identity: Wearing the Codpiece*. London: Palgrave Macmillan. Pp. 31–56.

LaPerle, C. M. (2021). Race in Shakespeare's tragedies. In A. Thompson (ed.), *The Cambridge Companion to Shakespeare and Race*. Cambridge: Cambridge University Press. Pp. 77–92.

Lister, D (1993). Was Shakespeare a Tory? The Bard is now a subject of political controversy. *Independent*, 3 January.

Leitch (2009). *Film Adaptation and Its Discontents: From* Gone with the Wind *to* The Passion of Christ. Baltimore, MD: Johns Hopkins University Press.

Marenbon, J. (1987). *English Our English: The New Orthodoxy Examined*. London: Centre for Policy Studies.

Marshall, B. (2000). *English Teachers: The Unofficial Guide. Researching the Philosophies of English Teachers*. London: Routledge Falmer.

Marshall, B. (2003). The write kind of knowledge in English. *Critical Quarterly* 45(4), 113–25.

Marshall, B. (2020). Reading the canon via synthetic phonics: Texts as political pawns. In B. Marshall, J. Manuel, D. Pasternak and J. Rowsell (eds.), *The Bloomsbury Handbook of Reading Perspectives and Practices*. London: Bloomsbury.

The Mastery Curriculum (2019). www.englishmastery.org/programme. Accessed 10 June 2019.

Morgan, W. and C. M. Wyatt-Smith (2000). Im/proper accountability: Towards a theory of critical literacy and assessment. *Assessment in Education: Principles, Policy & Practice* 7(1), 123–42.

Morrison, T. (1993). *Playing in the Dark*. New York: Vintage.

Pascall, D. (1992). The cultural dimension in education. *The Royal Society of Arts*. London: The National Foundation for Arts Education.

Patten, J. (1992). Speech at the Conservative Party Conference.

Pearson, Edexcel (2017). *Pearson Edexcel Level 3 Advanced GCE in English Literature (9ET0) Sample Assessment Materials First Certification 2017 Issue 5.* https://qualifications.pearson.com/content/dam/pdf/A%20Level/English%20Literature/2015/Specification%20and%20sample%20assessments/A-English-Literature-issue-5.pdf. Accessed 15 December 2021.

Pimlico Academy (2019). www.pimlicoacademy.org/page/?title=Our+Curriculum&pid=20 Accessed 10 June 2019.

Pratt, M. (1986). Interpretive strategies/strategic interpretations on Anglo-American reader response criticism. In J. Arac (ed.), *Postmodernism and Politics*. Minneapolis: University of Minnesota Press. Pp. 26–54.

Reynolds, P. (1991). Unlocking the box: Shakespeare on film and video. In L. Aers and N. Wheale (eds.), *Shakespeare in the Changing Curriculum*. London: Routledge.

Rosenshine, B. (2012). *Principles of Instruction: Research-Based Strategies That All Teachers Should Know*. Springer: American Educator.

Shakespeare, W. *Macbeth* (2016). Directed by Justin Audibert. The National Theatre, London.

Shakespeare, W. *Romeo and Juliet* (2016). Directed by Beijan Sheibani. The National Theatre, London.

Smith, E. (ed.). (2021). *Shakespeare Survey 74: Shakespeare and Education*. Cambridge: Cambridge University Press.

Thompson, A. (2011). *Passing Strange: Shakespeare, Race and Contemporary America*. Oxford: Oxford University Press.

Thompson, A. (2017). How should we listen to Audiences? Race, reception, and the audience survey. In J. C. Bulman (ed.), *The Oxford Handbook of Shakespeare and Performance*. Oxford: Oxford University Press. Pp. 1–14.

Thompson, A. (ed.) (2021). *The Cambridge Companion to Shakespeare and Race*. Cambridge: Cambridge University Press.

Willingham, D. (2009). *Why Don't Students Like School? A Cognitive Scientist Answers Questions about How the Mind Works and What It Means for Your Classroom*. San Francisco, CA: Jossey-Bass.

Wood, M. (2017). *On Empson*. Princeton, NJ. Princeton University Press.

Wyatt-Smith, C., and J. Murphy (2001). What counts as writing assessment? An Australian move to mainstream critical literacy. *English and Education* 35(1), 12–32.

Yandell, J (2001). What's in a name, or electric cars for all. *Changing English* 8(2), 145–54.

Yandell, J. (2013). The social construction of meaning: Reading *Animal Farm* in the classroom. *Literacy* 47(1), 50–5.

Yandell, J. (2017). Culture, knowledge and power: What the Conservatives have learnt from E. D. Hirsch. *Changing English* 24(3), 246–52.

Yandell, J. (2020). Reader response in the classroom. In B. Marshall, J. Manuel, D. Pasternak and J. Rowsell (eds.), *The Bloomsbury Handbook of Reading Perspectives and Practices*. London: Bloomsbury.

Yandell, J., and Brady, M. (2016). English and the politics of knowledge. *English in Education* 50(1), 44–59.

Young, H. (2010). *Embodying Black Experience: Stillness, Critical Memory, and the Black Body*. Ann Arbor: University of Michigan Press (ACLS Humanities E-Book).

Young, M. (2013). Overcoming the crisis in curriculum theory: A knowledge-based approach. *Journal of Curriculum Studies* 45(2), 101–18.

Young, M., and D. Lambert, with C. Roberts and M. Roberts (2014). *Knowledge and the Future School: Curriculum and Social Justice*. London: Bloomsbury.

Filmography

Hamlet (1948). Directed by Laurence Olivier [Film] UK, Rank Films Distributors Ltd.

Hamlet (1990). Directed by Franco Zeffirelli [Film] UK, Guild Film Distribution.

Hamlet (1996). Directed by Kenneth Branagh [Film] UK, Rank Films Distributors Ltd.

Hamlet (2009). Directed by Gregory Doran [Film] UK, BBC.

Hamlet (2018). Directed by Rhodri Huw, Robert Icke [Filmed Stage Production] UK, Almeida Film Production.

Cambridge Elements ⁼

Shakespeare and Pedagogy

Liam E. Semler
The University of Sydney

Liam E. Semler is Professor of Early Modern Literature in the Department of English at the University of Sydney. He is author of *Teaching Shakespeare and Marlowe: Learning versus the System* (2013) and co-editor (with Kate Flaherty and Penny Gay) of *Teaching Shakespeare beyond the Centre: Australasian Perspectives* (2013). He is editor of *Coriolanus: A Critical Reader* (2021) and co-editor (with Claire Hansen and Jackie Manuel) of *Reimagining Shakespeare Education: Teaching and Learning through Collaboration* (Cambridge, 2023). His most recent book outside Shakespeare studies is *The Early Modern Grotesque: English Sources and Documents 1500–1700* (2019). Liam leads the Better Strangers project which hosts the open-access Shakespeare Reloaded website (shakespearereloaded.edu.au).

Gillian Woods
Birkbeck College, University of London

Gillian Woods is Reader in Renaissance Literature and Theatre at Birkbeck College, University of London. She is the author of *Shakespeare's Unreformed Fictions* (2013; joint winner of Shakespeare's Globe Book Award), *Romeo and Juliet: A Reader's Guide to Essential Criticism* (2012), and numerous articles about Renaissance drama. She is the co-editor (with Sarah Dustagheer) of *Stage Directions and Shakespearean Theatre* (2018). She is currently working on a new edition of *A Midsummer Night's Dream* for Cambridge University Press, as well as a

Leverhulme-funded monograph about Renaissance Theatricalities. As founding director of the Shakespeare Teachers' Conversations, she runs a seminar series that brings together university academics, school teachers and educationalists from non-traditional sectors, and she regularly runs workshops for schools.

ADVISORY BOARD

Janelle Jenstad, University of Victoria

Farah Karim-Cooper, Shakespeare's Globe

Bi-qi Beatrice Lei, National Taiwan University

Florence March, Université Paul-Valéry Montpellier

Peggy O'Brien, Folger Shakespeare Library

Paul Prescott, University of California Merced

Abigail Rokison-Woodall, University of Birmingham

Emma Smith, University of Oxford

Patrick Spottiswoode, Shakespeare's Globe

Jenny Stevens, English Association

Ayanna Thompson, Arizona State University

Joe Winston, University of Warwick

ABOUT THE SERIES

The teaching and learning of Shakespeare around the world is complex and changing. Elements in Shakespeare and Pedagogy synthesises theory and practice, including provocative, original pieces of research, as well as dynamic, practical engagements with learning contexts.

Cambridge Elements ☰

Shakespeare and Pedagogy

The Pedagogy of Watching Shakespeare
Bethan Marshall, Myfanwy Edwards and Charlotte Dixey

A full series listing is available at: www.cambridge.org/ESPG

Printed in the United States
by Baker & Taylor Publisher Services